Game Mods: Design, Theory and Criticism

Game Mods:

Design, Theory and Criticism

edited by Erik Champion

Table of Contents

Mod

Mod

Glorious Mod

Erik Champion

10

Introduction: Mod Mod Glorious Mod

Erik Champion, Digital Humanities Lab Denmark,
IT-Parken, Wienerbygningen, Helsingforsgade 14,
8200 Aarhus N, Aarhus University,
echa@adm.au.dk

"Dismiss this, it's just about mods!" This sentence was a comment a reviewer wrote on an early conference paper submission. The subtext was clear to me, the writer. Rather than say the paper was substandard (which may well have been the case), the reviewer could not imagine that discussing game mods could be of any value to an academic audience. Well I don't know who the reviewer was so I am briefly going to inflict my retort on you, gentle reader.

Firstly it never hurts for theorists to get elbow deep in practice, just as it does not hurt for a practitioner to encounter, experience and test a little theory. In my experience from running game design classes, even professional gamers learn a great deal from discussing and debating game design, both the successes and the failures.

My students may well complain that I intellectualize, but even the most intellectual of game theorists can learn from the actual process of game design, and from watching people play. Theorists learn about the entangled issues of game design, the politics of user testing, and the designer fallacy (I designed the game, I know how best to experience it, if the audience can't work it out there is something wrong with them, not the design). Practitioners in turn can begin to understand (perhaps) how theory, good theory, can help open eyes, inspire new design and turn description into prescription. Granted, even theorists can get confused between describing a good game and prescribing what makes a good game, but it is an excellent way of thinking more deeply about why good games work, and whether breaking down their success into rules, guidelines or patterns can actually create more good games.

What are mods? According to Finch (2011) and Wikipedia (2012), "Mods, short for 'modifications' are user-made edits made to PC videogames..." We will take a wider view of mods in this book, but Finch's (2011) definition is a reasonable starting point:

What is a mod? Mods, short for 'modifications', are user-made edits made to PC videogames, the game equivalent of fan fiction. Traditionally free, they range from minor code changes to fix bugs or smoothen gameplay to 'total conversions'—complete overhauls of art assets to form an entirely new experience.

A computer itself could be considered "modded" (O'Brien, 2012), but none of the authors in this book seem to take this definition. Game modifications can be artwork, skins (graphic look), tools, total game transformations, new code, or, perhaps less clearly, games ported to other platforms by fans. They can also be homage games, which link back to earlier separate, but thematically-linked game worlds. These are not necessarily mods in a strict sense. The endgame, rather than higher, locked levels, could be the modding itself, to extend and expand the enjoyment of the game. In a similar vein, Scacchi (2010) proposed five types of game mods: user interface customizations, game conversions, machinima and art mods, game computer customization, and game console hacking.

In "Am I Mod or Not? - an Analysis of First Person Shooter Modification Culture" Nieborg (2005, p.11) suggested exact definitions would not be forthcoming:

> Although both gamers and scholars do not have any
> trouble with the term 'mod' and seem to share a
> common understanding of what is or what is not a mod,
> the question whether a game is a mod or a "regular"
> (commercial) game is an arbitrary one.

"Arbitrary" is a strong word, but it is true that the semantic distinctions between a tool to create mods, an editor to design or save levels, and the distinction between a partial mod and a total mod, are all contestable. What exactly are the criteria by which a modification to a game can be considered to be a game mod? Merely changing keyboard shortcuts is not enough; a game mod in this day and age seems to be less and less any incremental additions or deletions to a game level, and more and more a noticeable and significantly intentional change to the gameplay and experience of the game itself. And the audience for game mods is increasingly demanding (Totilo, 2011). Unfortunately we don't yet have terms to distinguish between games that have been personalized or otherwise incrementally altered, games that have been significantly created ex nihilo, and game mods that provoke and challenge our notion of the original games or of the gameplay itself (Laukkanen, 2005).

If not a pedigree, at least mods have some form of a history; they have been around for a good three, four, even five decades. In this book Peter Christiansen argues that *SpaceWar!* (1962) was the first game mod. It was at least a good sign of hacking culture (Laukkanen, 2005). And that is half a century before the release of this book. Of course there is debate over the first mod, Bogacs (2008) named the 1983 game *Lode Runner* as the first game with a game editor, but he seemed to think *Ms. Pac-Man* was the first game mod, created in 1981 and released in 1982. More recently, *ZZTT* (1991) was a text program with an editor; it spawned many mods (Au, 2002). Au noted that by 1993 there was also a *Castle Smurfenstein*, a humorous mod of *Castle Wolfenstein*, where all the Nazis were replaced by Smurfs. Some of the original files are still online (Johnson, n.d.).

Arguably, it was *DOOM*, released in 1993 by id Software, which was not just a pioneering First Person Shooter 3D game, but also the first game to be deliberately designed for modmaking. The company released WADs (Where's All the Data?) mods; the *Doom Editing Utility* (DEU) software and later *The Doom Construction Kit: Mastering and Modifying Doom*, and a free version of *DOOM* that was downloaded over 10 million times.

For turn-based games, Lochutus (2010) dates Civ-modmaking back to 1991 for *Civilization I*, but as a "mainstream phenomenon" (and the development of modding communities) to 1996 for *Civilization II*. Quite possibly the first hack-modded turn-based game was *Empire* or *Classic Empire*, originally written by Walter Bright, and released in 1977, (Godfellow, 2006). It was not intended for modding, the mods and ported version were distributed, if not altogether legally, and modding it inspired the lead designer of *Civilization II* to promote modding features with *Civ II*, even if he had to disobey his own company to do so (Godfellow, 2006).

Why design mods? Mods can extend the life of the original game, and inspire the professional game designers and owners of the original franchise. Au (2002) wrote:

> Player-created additions to computer games aren't a hobby anymore -- they're the lifeblood of the industry.. Miller and his "Wolf3D" developers watched astounded as mods "actually helped extend the life of a game by providing free additional content for players to explore.

Brian Reynolds, the lead designer of *Civilization II* (and a self-confessed hacker or modder of *Empire*) risked the displeasure of his employers in creating scenarios for *Civ II* modders. In a fascinating online interview with Troy Godfellow (2006) he noted:

> Much of the "viral marketing" we got for Civ2 in the first year came from the power of the scenario & mod community. The mods & scenarios also made the Civ2 expansion packs possible, and these in turn kept the franchise going strong for the full five years until the release of Civ3 – you could still find Civ2 selling for a strong price in any game store right up until Civ3 shipped. Indeed, scenarios and modability are now cornerstones of the whole franchise – every Civ generation gets multiple X-packs and the modability just becomes more and more detailed. So truly I think the scenarios and [sic] modabilty have proven key not just to Civ2 specifically but to the whole Civ franchise (and I'll happily take credit for defiantly taking the first step against orders, one of my last great feats of "commando programming"!)

Although adding modding scenarios to *Civilization II* was a dangerous career move for Reynolds, (but a huge factor in the ongoing success of the game franchise), mod design can be also be the entry ticket into a professional job in the game industry. Perry (n.d.) asked Valve founder Gabe Newell how to get a job, considering how tough it was to break into the industry with no prior experience. Newell replied "The best thing to do is to start making content using the MOD tools that are out there."

The foot in the door can be for mod tool design as well. Robert Duffy was so frustrated by the *QuakeEd* level editor for id Software's *Quake II*, that he offered his own improved version for free on his website. This piece of altruism was not overlooked; he was offered a job over the phone by id Software's cofounder, John Carmack (Au, 2002).

Game companies know that their modding tools are also interview resources, and business products. Gary Newman, the inventor of the famous modding tool, *Gary's mod*, flunked his own job interview with Valve, (Totilo, 2010), but he still managed to sell his add-on tool over a million times (Senior, 2012). As Newman mentioned to Totilo, modding is no longer simple and amateurish, it is a serious business, and a popular hobby. Nardi and Kallinikos (2007) note that "CTMod claims over one hundred million downloads—an astonishing figure for any software."

Large scale mod design involves vast amount of people management, and can lead to jobs in non-gaming industries. For example, *Nehrim* (Sureai, n.d.), is a complete game conversion of *Elder Scrolls IV: Oblivion*. The designers claim it is a totally new story and characters, and features original music and 56 professional voice actors, all recorded in a professional recording studio in Berlin. Although I cannot guarantee the modders scored recording contracts, has anyone heard of "Mages' Got Talent"?

Apart from increasing one's employment prospects, designing a game mod is one of the few fields of criticism where one can design and test an alternative to the current offering from the comfort of an armchair. Joubert (2010) noted:

> Since time immemorial, players have looked at the games they've played and decided that they could do one better. It's the classic scenario which begins with a humble "what if?" and eventually turns into a vast community-driven spectacular of custom content, innovative ideas and foul-tempered 13-year-olds trying to blast each other with AKs.

Are mods quality products? Mods are not necessarily low-quality. Will Wright has remarked on their creativity (Au, 2002), Scacchi (2011) has remarked on their use as "a leading form of user-led innovation in game design and game play experience". And Bethesda, the makers of the *Elder Scrolls* series, wrote in 2011 on their blog:

> Bethesda has a long history of supporting the modding community, and for good reason. It's a science fact that mod tools make the world a better place: they make modders happy because they can mod, they make developers happy to see modders gaining experience, and they make fans happy to see an endless stream of content they can mess around with.

Quantity is not always quality, but there is an argument to be made that many in the modding community believe some mods are as well designed as the original games (Fomin, 2012). Mods can target more specialized audiences, and thus can (sometimes) create a more thoughtful and authentic experience than the actual game they originated from, they can be a reflexive experience (Nardi and Kallinikos, 2007). Au (2002) wrote "while the professional WWII games are quite good in their own right, their believability is marred by the assumptions of mass market and the clichés of the first-person shooter genre". He noted that some mods have no onscreen bloodshed, unlike the original games.

Further, Au (2002) remarked: "mods can come up with new gameplay elements that the industry is too conservative to implement, or non-creative to come up with." Two examples of Battlefield mods with an original theme are *Siege* (Siege mod team, 2003) and *Battlefield Pirates* (Scurvy Cove Productions, 2003).

Nardi and Kallinikos argued that despite limited tools, modding in World of Warcraft can greatly improve the user experience:

> However, the quality of play—the user experience—is vastly changed through the use of mods. Mods reduce effort, make visible invisible parts of the game, aid players in coordinating with one another, and capture important aspects of a player's history of play.

Au (2002) suggested that one way of comparing the quality of mods is on authenticity, on how well it compares to the original historical event or situation. Judged on historical authenticity and battlefield realism, *Day of Defeat* is actually better than both of them, treating the grim nature of World War II with the fidelity it deserves. "The ultimate compliment for us," says Thornton, "is when veterans of military service play our game and say, 'That's just what it's like!'"

In his online blog piece, "The Top 10 Game Mods Of All Time," Finch (2011) proposed various criteria for judging the aesthetic value of mods. By best, he appears to mean most influential in the gaming community. But he also listed the following attributes: atmosphere (such as in *Aliens TC*), innovative gameplay and genuine team work (*Team Fortress*), inventive and creative (*Chaos DM*), populist appeal (*Counter Strike*), and also incredible popularity (*Defense of the Ancients*, with 20 million players in China alone), path-finding "gritty realism" (*Red Orchestra*), the most successful indie project on *Steam* (*Garry's Mod*), and one without selection criteria listed unless you count "a story-driven experimental ghost story" (*Dear Esther*). He also quoted Bethesda's compliment to the *Cube Experimental* mod, "one of the most impressive mods for *Fallout 3*" (*CUBE Experimental*), while *Black Mesa* contained "an exhaustive overhaul of detailed art assets." So for Finch, mods can be judged on their atmosphere, gameplay, popularity, gritty realism, transmedial innovation, or sheer amount of work undertaken.

Wawro and Miller (2011) used similar criteria for their sixteen best mods, they wrote "Valve Software elevated the first-person shooter to a narrative style with the debut of *Half-Life*," and they also seem to value games that were modded to reflect completely different genres and gameplay. In passing they also mention how one *Elder Scrolls III: Morrowind* mod has a complete environment modeled by fans' imagination as to the back history of the entire *Elder Scrolls* universe. The one unique feature they mention is not really a mod, or is it? In the original *Half-Life* game one can choose between a gun or a flashlight, but not both. In this mod, there is duct tape to tie the gun to the light so the player does not have to shoot in darkness. Considering the setting is a research complex, duct tape makes sense, but affects the gameplay (now the game is far less scary). It is arguably the only example listed by critics where modding has to balance immersion versus in-world realism.

A similar online article by Fahey (2011) also featured the same criteria. Kenney's 2011 article on the most significant 15 mods (although entitled modders, it refers to the mods themselves), also emphasized the importance of completeness and immersivity, and the ability to combine several game genres in the one game. Senior's 2010 article on the ten most "essential" *Oblivion* mods favored those which adjusted gameplay, had a greater amount of detail, and evoked a rich sense of atmosphere.

The online article by Hatfield (2012), "The 25 best Skyrim Mods," mostly ranked and judged mods on how far they could either redress *Skyrim* issues or add aesthetic effects. He also mentioned a mod by an arachnophobe that was designed to remove all spiders from the game, but the replacements were giant bears that appeared in the most inappropriate places. So mods can be selected for unexpected humor, but generally the way in which mods were judged appears to be mostly on account of popularity, additional detail they add to textures and atmospheric effects, homages such as games within games or games recreated in a completely different game engine, or improvements to user interface and game balance issues.

There is however some debate as to whether greater progress was made in terms of products (the mods) or the process (the tools designed in order to create the mods). In his short online article, Locklear (2002) argued that the real stars of modding are the toolmakers rather than the modders themselves. Apart from the issue of modding tools versus mods, very few of these awards and rankings seem to have been based on how the mod provokes us or challenges convention.

There are reflexive games and reflexive game mods. The game *September 12*, inspired a Socratic debate between a philosopher and a digital humanist (Rockwell and Kee, 2011), *Space Refugees* was almost a game mod, a thoughtful agency-reversing homage to space invader games, (Whalen, n.d.);

and *Escape from Woomera*, a game mod, was a semi-ludic criticism of refugee policy in Australia that infuriated the then government minister (Nicholls, 2003). At least one home-made mod has accidentally threatened and humiliated US intelligence services, Congress and mainstream media (*Sonic Jihad*, see Losh, 2007); yet much more debate seems to focus on games per se rather than on modding. There is still room to develop more reflexive mods, and to further develop game mod criticism.

While it appears that modding is an excellent way for a player to personalize and customize their gameplay, Nardi and Kallinikos put forward an interesting ethical and legal question. On pages 12-13 they wrote:

> Mods, then, are a creative means by which to make a game fit players' interests, values, feelings, and orientations in pleasing ways. Mods go some distance toward allowing players' personalities to shape experience with a software artifact... In other words; are we witnessing the rise and subsequent fall of FPS mod culture based on an open-source ethos or are we at the beginning of a new era featuring cleverly commoditised user-created content?

In "Am I mod or not", Nieborg (2005) also warned us that "the bottom-up practice of developing mods is collaborative in nature and in certain cases somewhat artificially created. There is an absence of criticism on the rise of commodification practices within gaming culture." He also noted in another publication (2007) that "A lot of digitized information seems to be up for grabs. Leadbeater's model of mass creativity equals constant unpaid labor by the masses but not so much for the masses." These issues have come to the attention of not just game design academics (Kücklich, 2005) but also business academics (Jeppesen, 2004).

In our first chapter, "Between a Mod and a Hard Place," Peter Christiansen elaborates on why people design mods, the value of modding, and how modding is carried out so as not to raise the ire of game developers. For example, he refers to *SpaceWar!* as the first game mod. Christiansen pronounces it significant not because of technical achievement, but because it was never a commodity. It was never sold, mass-produced, or underwent copyright protection. The freedom of content creation possible with game modding leads to his observation that "modding allows people to make the games that the industry is not making." The "counter-hegemonic process" that he believes is possible with game modding is perhaps still to be fully realized, for the very people who could pay for the computer games featuring alternative interpretations of the gaming industry tend to be the very demographic that is the target of the alternative viewpoints. One example Christiansen gives is *Finnwars*, a *Battlefield* mod *[http://www.moddb.com/ mods/finnwars]*. The Finnish mod is a replay of three wars Finland fought (with the USSR and with Nazi Germany), but a period of history not well known or remembered in the West. This mod saw the development of a standalone game, *FinnWars II [http://www.iceflakestudios.com/fw2static/]*.

In Chapter 2, Natalie Underberg explains the design of a game mod, *Turkey Maiden Educational Computer Game,* to teach about Depression-era Ybor City, Florida history and culture. The area is known for its historic cigar industry and Latin immigrant population. The game itself is based on a Spanish folktale collected from Ybor City, Florida and was adapted into a video game mod using the popular Role Playing Game (RPG) *Neverwinter Nights*.

"Use of 'The Elder Scrolls Construction Set' to create a virtual history lesson", by Eric Fassbender, is our third chapter. In it, Fassbender describes his use of the level editor *Elder Scrolls Construction Set* (TESCS), to create a history tour of Macquarie Lighthouse, possibly the first lighthouse in the Southern Hemisphere. The mod was based on municipal blueprints, the 3D assets were imported into TESCS from 3D Studio max via a *Civilization* plugin (modders are used to these unusual software workflows), and Fassbender carefully outlines the steps required to create his mod and the avatar guide, (featuring lip-synched spoken information on the Lighthouse), all of which was then displayed on Macquarie University Reality Centre's three monitor display and immersive projection screen. *Oblivion's* TESCS is a powerful but easy tool to create complete mods that include realistic avatars and lip-synched verbal conversation. It can also feature some interesting musical accompaniments (which was the focus of Fassbinder's research). As a spatial visualization tool, it has been used for creating virtual buildings and cities by architects and urban designers (Varney, 2007).

One architect, Andrew Smith, of CASA at the University of London, said in Varney's 2007 article for The Escapist that "only when they [architects] actually see the work that they realize the power and potential of gaming for architectural visualization. As such, most of the work is carried out by the modding community, rather than academics or professionals." His viewpoint is seconded by Chris Totten, who with some advice from Valve level designer Chris Chin, wrote his Master's thesis on how game design can help architectural design (Gamasutra staff, 2009) and a later article on how architectural design can help game mod design (Totten, 2010). So where does one start? Kevin Conway's Chapter 4, "Game Mods, Engines and Architecture", undertakes an introduction of some of the features of game design, particularly level design, and he discusses the pros and cons of mods for architectural visualization, ending with examples of a Bruce Goff House (Bruce Goff houses are a good challenge for 3D modeling, as they were known for their idiosyncratic and "organic" design).

There are many issues here which deserve further inspection; such as, which techniques of place making can help level design? How do architects address and extend the art of interactivity in a digital medium? Since the above essays, is architectural visualization via game engines now seen as a reputable pursuit by professional architects? Are they satisfied with the levels of graphic fidelity and amount of realistic detail? These issues are also of interest to other designers, from designers of human computer interaction, to designers of Virtual Reality environments.

In Chapter 5, "Teaching Mods with Class", I was interested in how students could learn about game design issues through level design, and modding allowed them to build complete levels within a single semester course. I was also very interested in how the design briefs I gave them, along with the ambitious design goals they had, if any genuinely creative and engaging solutions could emerge in the time given. So in this chapter I predominantly discuss game mods my students have created, but I also give some of my thoughts on what is best to focus on or to avoid in class, and ideas on how modding can be seen not only as an in-game level modification, but also as a way of modifying the game environment itself where even if the software is not directly modified, the agency, interface, and cultural design is significantly impacted.

Are mods creative? Although I may have touched on creative aspects of modding in my own chapter, there is no chapter directly on this issue, (at least not yet), as to whether game mods can be seen as creative, and there is no chapter on the related issue as to how to judge the aesthetic values (and perhaps categories) of game mods. Can there be a masterpiece mod? As I indicated earlier, mod theory is not the most detailed part of game studies, and the lack of a thorough response to these questions intrigues and infuriates me.

However, I can say that mods are definitely used creatively by design professionals. We don't have a chapter on game mods for art, (for that you might want to read the thesis by Bogacs, 2008). However, we do have a chapter on game mods for film-making. "Choosing a game and game engine for modding", by Friedrich Kirschner; examines some of the theoretical and conceptual ways in which mods can be used, perhaps you would like to create your own film. Kirschner reviews the histories and theories entangled up with machinima (game engines used and modified to make films). He explains his own design approach to a machinima competition, the mod itself, and the modding tools that he designed to help create his mod. Although this chapter may appear to be discussing practical matters, it is also a theoretical exposition on machinima as process rather than as product, and its position within game design and game studies.

Until Virtual Reality (VR) pills are available on prescription from the local pharmacist, the closest most of us will get to VR is probably via a large multi-wall installation, a CAVE. In Chapter 7, "CryVE: Modding the CryEngine2 to create a CAVE system", the final chapter, the authors Marija Nakevska, Alex Juarez, and Jun Hu, take us through the use of the *Crysis* engine to create a *CryVE*. A *CryVE* is a virtual environment (VE) created by projecting onto multiple walls game levels running inside a *CryEngine* game engine. This project is derived, at least in part from *CAVE UT*, and the original CAVE projects (multi wall VR projection system). The authors provide code and pseudo-code so you can run *CryEngine* and *CryEngine* mods as large-scale interactive projections, and they also give examples of mods that take advantage of such large surround spaces.

If you are interested in how researchers use other game engines to create multiwall or surround screen environments, you might also like to check out *http:/publicVR.org,* the website of Jeffrey Jacobson (the inventor of CAVE UT). The publicVR website includes free downloadable models and levels, but if you are also interested in projection calculations I recommend *http:// paulbourke.net/,* the website of visualization scientist Paul Bourke. His website describes in some detail how to design low-cost multiwall and curved screen projections for planetariums and domes using game engines and real-time rendering engines such as *Source (Half-Life 2), Blender,* and *Unity.*

To cut to the chase, there are many critical and theoretical and design-related issues lurking beneath the surface of game mods. Critical issues range from how to judge the aesthetic, technical and social values of game mods, to how or even whether one can construct general principles of criticism that can be applied to the judgment of game mods. Would this differ significantly from criticism in game studies? Are the theoretical issues involved in game mods merely a subset of game design theory, or something else? Should one reference or pay homage to the original game, can a designer display genuine innovation and creativity in the design of a mod? Could the design of game mods, and the design of tools to create game mods, be improved through criticism and theory? Are these toolsets useful and usable in teaching? And can the tools and techniques of game mod design be applied in areas beyond computer games? In the following chapters we touch on many of these issues, but we may well raise more questions than answers, the work has just begun!

References

Au, W.J (2002). Triumph of the mod. In *Salon*. [Electronic version]. Retrieved 1 May 2012, from *http://www.salon.com/2002/04/16/modding/*

Bethesda. (2011). New Creation Kit to bring modding tools to Skyrim. In *Bethblog (Bethesda blog)*. Electronic version]. Retrieved 1 May 2012, from http://www.bethblog.com/2011/01/19/new-creation-kit-to-bring-modding-tools-to-skyrim/

Bogacs, H. (2008). Game mods; a survey of modifications, appropriation and videogame art. Bachelor Thesis, Vienna University of Technology, Vienna. [Electronic version]. Retrieved 1 May 2012, from http://web.student.tuwien.ac.at/~e0326417/game_mods/game_mods.pdf

Fahey, M. (2011). These Are the Best PC Game Mods of 2011. In *Kotaku*. [Electronic version]. Retrieved 1 May 2012, from http://kotaku.com/5871352/these-are-the-best-pc-game-mods-of-2011

Finch, G. (2011). The Top 10 Game Mods Of All Time. In *The creators project (blog)*. [Electronic version]. Retrieved 1 May 2012, from http://www.thecreatorsproject.com/blog/the-top-10-game-mods-of-all-time

Fomin, E. (2012). Best Game Mods. In *UGO.com*. [Electronic version]. Retrieved 1 May 2012, from http://www.ugo.com/games/best-game-mods

Gamasutra Staff. (2009). GameCareerGuide: Game Design And Architecture. In *Gamasutra*. [Electronic version]. Retrieved 1 May 2012, from http://www.gamasutra.com/php-bin/news_index.php?story=24065

Godfellow, T. (2006). Civilization Chronicles Interview with Brian Reynolds. In *Civfanatics*. [Electronic version]. Retrieved 1 May 2012, from http://www.civfanatics.com/interviews/CivChronicles_Brian_Reynolds.php

Hatfield, T. (2012). The 25 best Skyrim Mods. In PC Gamer. [Electronic version]. Retrieved 1 May 2012, from http://www.pcgamer.

com/2012/01/17/the-25-best-skyrim-mods/

Jeppesen, L. B. (2004). *Profiting from innovative user communities: How firms organize the production of user modifications in the computer games industry.* København: Department of Strategic Management and Globalization. Copenhagen Business School. (Working paper). [Electronic version].http://www.evl.uic.edu/index.php Retrieved 1 May 2012, from http://research.cbs.dk/da/publications/profiting-from-innovative-user-communities(6ea9f480-c020-11db-9769-000ea68e967b).html

Johnson, A. (n.d.) The first 'Official' Castle Smurfenstein Home Page. In andy's page. http://www.evl.uic.edu/aej/smurf.html

Joubert, R. (2010). A (REALLY) BRIEF HISTORY OF GAME MODDING. In *NAG online.* [Electronic version]. Retrieved 1 May 2012, from http://www.nag.co.za/2009/03/19/a-really-brief-history-of-game-modding/. Posted Mar 19, 2009, last updated Jan 07, 2010.

Kenny, W. (2010). 15 Modders who changed PC gaming. In *GamingBolt.com: Video Game News, Reviews, Previews and Blog.* [Electronic version]. Retrieved 1 May 2012, from http://gamingbolt.com/15-modders-who-changed-pc-gaming

Kücklich, J. (2005). Precarious Playbour: Modders and the Digital Games Industry. In *The FibreCulture Journal, 5; Precarious Labour.* [Electronic version]. Retrieved 1 May 2012, from http://five.fibreculturejournal.org/fcj-025-precarious-playbour-modders-and-the-digital-games-industry/

Laukkanen, T. (2005). Modding Scenes. Introduction to User-created content in computer gaming. [Electronic version]. Retrieved 1 May 2012, from http://tampub.uta.fi/tup/951-44-6448-6.pdf Hypermedia Laboratory, net series 9.

Lochutus. (2010). A brief history of Civ modding (pt 1). In *Weplayciv* (online forum). [Electronic version]. Retrieved 1 May 2012, from http://www.weplayciv.com/forums/entry.php?5-A-brief-history-of-Civ-modding-(pt-1)

Locklear, F. (2002). It's a Mod Mod Mod Mod World. In *arstechnica.* [Electronic version]. Retrieved 1 May 2012, from http://arstechnica.com/uncategorized/2002/04/2200-2/

Losh, E. (2007). Artificial Intelligence, Media Illiteracy and the SonicJihad

23

Debacle in Congress. In *Media / Culture Journal*, 10(5). [Electronic version]. Retrieved 1 May 2012, from http://journal.media-culture. org.au/0710/08-losh.php

Nardi, B., & Kallinikos, J. (2007). Opening the Black Box of Digital Technologies: Mods in World of Warcraft. *23rd EGOS Colloquium*. [Electronic version]. Retrieved 1 May 2012, from http://www. darrouzet-nardi.net/bonnie/Nardi_Kallinikos_EGOS_08.pdf

Nicholls, N. (2003). Ruddock fury over Woomera computer game. [Electronic version]. Retrieved 1 May 2012, from http://www.theage. com.au/articles/2003/04/29/1051381948773.html

Nieborg, D. B. (2005). "Am I Mod or Not? - an Analysis of First Person Shooter Modification Culture." Paper presented at Creative Gamers Seminar - Exploring Participatory Culture in Gaming. Hypermedia Laboratory (University of Tampere). [Electronic version]. Retrieved 1 May 2012, from http://www.gamespace.nl/content/ DBNieborg2005_CreativeGamers.pdf

Nieborg, D. B. (2007). In Search of a Disclaimer – Mass Creativity as a Business Model. [Electronic version]. In *Gamespace*. [Electronic version]. Retrieved 1 May 2012, from http://www.gamespace.nl/ content/2007_Insearchofadisclaimer_Nieborg.pdf

O'Brien, T. (2012). *First Trial Over Video Game Console Mods Begins*. In switched. [Electronic version]. Retrieved 1 May 2012, from http:// www.switched.com/2010/11/30/matthew-crippen-first-trial-video- game-console-modding/

Perry, D. (n.d.) Valve founder Gabe Newell (interview online). In *switched*. [Electronic version]. Retrieved 1 May 2012, from http://www. switched.com/2010/11/30/matthew-crippen-first-trial-video-game- console-modding/

Rockwell, G. M. & Kee, K. (2011). The Leisure of Serious Games: A Dialogue. Game Studies, 11 (2). [Electronic version]. Retrieved 1 May 2012, from http://gamestudies.org/1102/articles/geoffrey_ rockwell_kevin_kee

Scacchi, W. (2010). Computer game mods, modders, modding, and the mod scene. In *First Monday, 15(5)*. [Electronic version]. Retrieved 1 May 2012, from http://firstmonday.org/htbin/cgiwrap/bin/ojs/index.php/ fm/article/view/2965/2526

Scacchi, W. (2011). Modding as an Open Source Approach to Extending Computer Game Systems. In S. Hissam, B. Russo, M.G. de Mendonca Neto, and F. Kan (Eds.), Open Source Systems: Grounding Research, *Proc. 7th. IFIP Intern. Conf. Open Source Systems*, 62-74, IFIP ACIT 365, Salvador. [Electronic version]. Retrieved 1 May 2012, from http://www.ics.uci.edu/~wscacchi/Papers/New/Scacchi-OSS2011.pdf

Senior, T. (2010). Ten essential Oblivion mods. In *PCgamer*. [Electronic version]. Retrieved 1 May 2012, from http://www.pcgamer.com/2010/07/16/ten-essential-oblivion-mods/

Senior, T. (2012). Garry's Mod has sold 1.4 million copies, Garry releases sales history to prove it. In *PCgamer*. [Electronic version]. Retrieved 1 May 2012, from http://www.pcgamer.com/2012/03/16/garrys-mod-has-sold-1-4-million-copies-garry-releases-sales-history-to-prove-it/

Sureai, (n.d.). NEHRIM. In *nehrim*. [Electronic version]. Retrieved 1 May 2012, from http://www.nehrim.de/indexEV.html

Totilo, S. (2010). Meet Garry, The Guy Who Re-Made How We Re-Make PC Games. Kotaku. [Electronic version]. Retrieved 1 May 2012, from http://en.wikipedia.org/wiki/Mod_(video_gaming)

Totten, C. (2010). Towards a Digital Architecture. In *Gamasutra*. [Electronic version]. Retrieved 1 May 2012, from http://gamasutra.com/blogs/ChristopherTotten/20100611/87496/Towards_a_Digital_Architecture.php

Varney, A. (2007). London in Oblivion. In *The Escapist*. [Electronic version]. Retrieved 1 May 2012, from http://www.escapistmagazine.com/articles/view/issues/issue_109/1331-London-in-Oblivion

Wawro, A., & Miller. P. (2011). Top 16 PC Game Mods. In *PCWorld*. [Electronic version]. Retrieved 1 May 2012, from http://en.wikipedia.org/wiki/Mod_(video_gaming).

Wikipedia (2012). Mod (video gaming). In *Wikipedia*. [Electronic version]. Retrieved 1 May 2012, from http://en.wikipedia.org/wiki/Mod_(video_gaming)

Whalen, Z. (n.d.). *Space Refugees*. In *Gameology*. [Electronic version]. Retrieved 1 May 2012, from http://www.gameology.org/files/videos/refugees.html

Chapter 1

Between

a Mod

and a

Hard Place

27

Peter Christiansen

28

Between a Mod and a Hard Place

Peter Christiansen, University of Utah, Languages &
Communication Bldg 255 South Central Campus Dr
RM 2400 84112-0491, Peter.Christiansen@utah.edu

In 1996, the long-standing tradition of the cereal box prize took its first step into the digital age. That year, millions of boxes of Chex cereal were packaged not with a whistle or a decoder ring, but with a CD containing the game *Chex Quest*. Although similar "advergames" had been around since the days of the Atari 2600, *Chex Quest*, which was developed for Ralston Foods by a small company known as Digital Café, was the first game ever to be distributed through cereal boxes (Miller, 2008). As a marketing promotion it was a huge success, increasing the sales of Chex cereal 295 percent and earning a number of marketing awards (Promotion Marketing Association, 2005). As a game, it also received a substantial amount of praise. *Chex Quest* was notable for being non-violent, as well as for having 3D graphics that were considered fairly impressive for its time.

Although the idea of creating a free game that puts the player in the role of an anthropomorphic piece of cereal sounds ill-conceived at best, perhaps the most remarkable part of this story is the fact that unlike most games, *Chex Quest* was not built from scratch. Its developers had taken an existing game and modified it to suit their particular needs.

In actuality, *Chex Quest* was *Doom*.

To be more precise, *Chex Quest* was a *Doom* mod; a highly modified version of the controversial first-person shooter created by Id Software. Although the underlying game mechanics remained essentially unchanged, the team at Digital Café swapped out the graphics and sounds, replacing *Doom*'s zombies and demons with cartoon alien blobs. Pools of blood were replaced by bright green slime and weapons were replaced by wacky teleportation devices. The final product was a game so unlike the original, that even as *Doom* was becoming the target of lawsuits and protests due to its violent gameplay and satanic imagery (Kushner, 2003, pg 267-268), parents were being encouraged to go from supermarket to supermarket to get their hands on a copy of *Chex Quest* (Sloane, 1997).

Although mods are occasionally created by companies such as Digital Café,

29

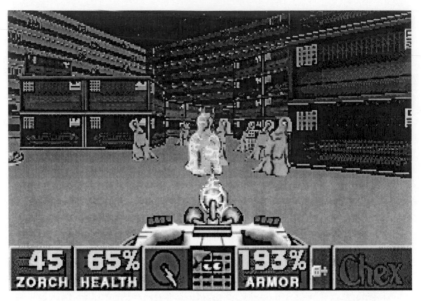

Figure 1: The game *Chex Quest* was included in boxes of Chex Cereal as part of a marketing campaign. The game itself was actually a mod of the game *Doom*.

the majority of modders are amateurs. They are players who want to take the experience of the game beyond its traditional constraints, becoming not just consumers of content, but producers as well (Jenkins, 2008, pg 162-164). Modding can be seen as a manifestation of the desire to tinker, to experiment with existing ideas and technologies in order to create something new. Online fan communities provide an environment conducive to this form of experimentation. These networks of dedicated players provide much more than just camaraderie. Members contribute large amounts of content to the community, ranging from hints to cheats to technical support. Modders both benefit from and add to this knowledge base, encouraging others to do the same (Postigo, 2003, pg 595-596). As modding has become more popular and the mods being created by these groups have grown in complexity, dedicated modding websites like ModDB and digital distribution services such as Valve's Steam have begun to appear. These sites host thousands of mods, as well as hundreds of tutorials to help aspiring modders get their start.

Creating a mod today is easier than it ever has been. Game mods are no longer the exclusive realm of brilliant hackers. Anyone with the desire and the willingness to learn can find the resources to make one. In addition to the online communities of modders that provide both information and resources for modding, more and more developers are making their tools available to modders, as well as incorporating mod-management tools in the commercial releases of many games.

Despite all these conveniences, being a modder is not as easy as it sounds. Though modding, in one form or another, has been around as long as computer games themselves, it occupies a somewhat precarious position within the videogame ecosystem. Modders are caught in the middle, somewhere between being normal players and being full-fledged developers. Their activities are subject to restrictions that don't apply to normal players, yet they aren't afforded the same rights that professional developers are. When it comes to the politics of the videogame industry, modders are often given the short end of the stick.

So is it worth it to become a modder? How does one go about making a mod without running afoul of game developers and publishers? What is it about modding that inspires so many people to devote so much time and effort to it? To address these questions, perhaps we should go back to the beginning...

A Brief History of Modding

Although there were a number of early experiments related to electronic games in the 1950's and 1960's, the one that would have the most significant impact on videogames as a medium was the game *Spacewar!*, created at MIT by Steve Russell. Russell, a member of the MIT Tech Model Railroad Club, wanted to create a game that could take advantage of the new PDP-1, the first computer at MIT to feature a monitor. Taking inspiration from a number of science fiction novels, he decided to create a game based around space combat (Kent, 2001, pg 17-18). *Spacewar!* would become one of the favorite pastimes among the hackers of the Tech Model Railroad Club and would soon spread to nearly every university in the country that had a computer lab. It would also become the general public's first exposure to videogames when in 1972, Stewart Brand organized the first "Intergalactic Spacewar Olympics" and documented the event in an article for *Rolling Stone Magazine* (Turner, 2006, pg 116).

Although the game itself is more closely related to modern videogames than any of the experiments that had come before, its cultural significance was very different. Unlike the majority of videogames created today, *Spacewar!* was never sold. It was never mass produced, nor was it even copyrighted – quite the opposite, in fact. The game's source code was spread from university to university along the primitive networks that would one day form the backbone of the early Internet. Russell and his fellow club members believed in the hacker ethic, that access to computers and information should be unlimited and total (Levy, 2010, pg 28). The motivation behind creating *Spacewar!* was sharing it with others.

The development of *Spacewar!* was also quite different from today's practices. Although Steve Russell programmed the core mechanics, other features were added by other members of the Tech Model Railroad Club. Pete Sampson added a program he dubbed "Expensive Planetarium" to generate stars for the background. Dan Edwards added functions for calculating gravity. Other hackers added a hyperspace button and even built primitive controllers out of scrounged parts (Kent, 2001, pg 19-20). The final version of *Spacewar!* was the product of a group effort by a team of hackers, each one working without pay to make his or her contribution to the final game. *Spacewar!* was not just the first computer game, it was also the first game to be modded.

Many early videogames would follow the model of *Spacewar!*, with groups of dedicated enthusiasts working together and sharing their code. Each game was both a piece of entertainment as well as a set of instructions for aspiring programmers. Most computers at the time, however, lacked the power of MIT's PDP-1. Many of these computers didn't even have monitors, let alone the ability to create real-time graphics. Undaunted, hackers soon began developing text-based games that could easily run on these machines.

One of the most influential text-based games ever made began as a spelunking game called *Colossal Cave Adventure*. It was a simple exploration game, in which the player explored a huge cavern finding items along the way. Its creator, Willie Crowther, had programmed it to understand simple commands like "GO NORTH," making it easy for even non-programmers to understand. The game was soon being passed from player to player across ARPANET, the predecessor of today's Internet (B. King and Borland, 2003, pg 30-31).

One such player was Don Woods, a computer science graduate student at Stanford. *Colossal Cave Adventure* was like no game he had ever seen. He was soon scouring ARPANET, searching for the game's creator. When he finally found Crowther, Woods asked him if he could modify the game. Crowther agreed, and Woods set about streamlining the code and adding all manner of puzzles and monsters. When he released his modified version, now titled simply *Adventure,* it became an instant success (B. King & Borland, 2003, pg 31-32). *Adventure* would go on to inspire a whole new genre of text-adventure games as well as a whole new generation of game developers (Levy, 1984, pg 295-302).

As the popularity of videogames spread, they soon transformed from a hobby into a thriving industry. No longer limited to a handful of high-tech university labs, videogames could be played in arcades across the world. Although an arcade cabinet was a big investment, most games would easily earn back their initial cost and go on on to make a considerable profit. Once a game began to wane in popularity, however, the cabinet was soon next to worthless.

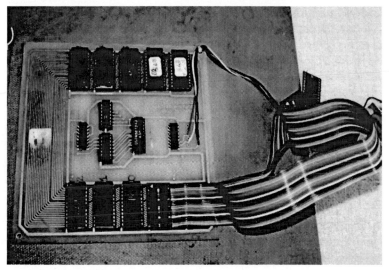

Figure 2: Unlike most mods, *Super Missile Attack* was a physical circuit board that was hard-wired into an existing *Missile Command* cabinet.

33

Seeing an opportunity in these old cabinets, Doug Macrae and Kevin Curran, a pair of MIT students, decided to bring new life to some of these old games. Their creation was a game called *Super Missile Attack*, an enhanced version of *Missile Command* that featured increased difficulty and even a few new enemies. Of course, modding an arcade game required a lot more than adding a few lines of code to a file. Their "mod" consisted of a custom circuit board designed to attach to the existing boards inside the cabinet. The new modded version became so popular that they began selling the boards, eventually shipping over a thousand copies (Kent, 2001, pg 167-169).

The success of *Super Missile Attack* had unintended consequences. When Atari, the creators of the original *Missile Command*, learned about Macrae and Curran's operation, they took the pair to court for copyright infringement. In the end, Atari dropped the suit and even agreed to pay them a settlement as long as they would stop selling their enhancement kits (Kent, 2001, pg 169-

170). The modders had survived their first clash with the law, but the *Super Missile Attack* incident proved that modding was a lot more complicated than just understanding the game's technology. To succeed at modding, you also had to understand the culture and the politics of the videogame industry.

With the advent of the Apple II, personal computers began to become commonplace in American households, creating a new space for videogames to flourish. Along with these new videogames came a new generation of modders, eager for a chance to experiment with the new technology. Among the first to do so were a pair of high school students, Andrew Johnson and Preston Nevins. Armed with a pair of Apple computers and a mutual hatred for The Smurfs, the two founded their own "development studio," Dead Smurf Software (Nevins, 1999).

Their first game, *Dino Smurf*, was a mod of *Dino Eggs*, by David H. Schroeder. Their tools were limited to basic file editing software, as well as a program that would dump the contents of a file to the graphics screen. Through trial and error, they were able to find the various game assets and replace them with Smurf-related content (Nevins, 1999).

For their second game, they chose a slightly more ambitious project, creating a mod of the popular Apple II game *Castle Wolfenstein*, by Silas Warner. *Castle Wolfenstein* was one of the first stealth-based games. The goal was to sneak through the castle, stealing uniforms and weapons, until you could find the Nazi battle plans. It was also notable for being the first Apple game to use digitized voices, with the guards shouting "Achtung" upon seeing you and "Kaputt" when you were caught (Warner, 1981).

Considering Nazis a less than relevant threat in the early 1980s, Johnson and Nevins once again replaced the graphics with Smurfs, creating *Castle Smurfenstein* (A. Johnson, 1996). With the help of a VCR and *The Voice*, the same program used to create the voices in the original game, the two even added some highly distorted Smurf voices. These games eventually became cult classics among Apple users. Their spread was such that even years after Johnson and Nevins had lost the original copies of the games, other copies surfaced on the Internet when Apple emulators began to gain in popularity (Nevins, 1999).

Perhaps the most influential figures in the history of modding were the founders of Id Software. Like the duo at Dead Smurf Software, the developers at Id took inspiration from Silas Warner's game, creating *Wolfenstein 3D*. Not long after the game's release, they found their code had already been hacked.

This time, the modders had chosen Barney the Dinosaur as the target of their wrath, substituting the children's television character for the final boss. Though several members of Id were concerned about copyright infringement, John Carmack and John Romero, two of the company's founders, were delighted to see modders experimenting with their code (Kushner, 2003, pg 115-116). At a time when most companies were still trying to sue modders, Id not only allowed them to carry on, they decided to help them.

With Id's next major release, *Doom,* the game was developed with modding in mind. All the parts of the program that modders needed to modify were put in external WAD (Where's All the Data?) files. Modders no longer had to overwrite the original game data in order to create a mod. All they had to do was have the program look at a different WAD and the game would load in the appropriate content (Kushner, 2003, pg 166).

35

Figure 3: Doom was one of the first games that was designed to be easily modded.

Almost twenty years later, there is still a large community of *Doom* modders. Of course, *Doom* was not the only game popular among modders in the 1990s. The growing availability of the Internet was making online collaboration possible on a much larger scale than ever before. This allowed for the creation and distribution of numerous fan-created modding tools.

These tools made it possible for modders to hack large, complex games like *StarCraft* (D. Johnson, 2009, pg 54). Even *Doom* modders benefited from fan made tools, such as DEU, the Doom Editor Utility, which was created by an international team of gamer led by Brendon Wyber, a college student in New Zealand (Kushner, 2003, pg 167-168).

The open nature of *Doom* inspired a flood of creativity among its fan community. Modders created mods themed around *Batman*, around *Star Trek*, and around the movie *Aliens*. Some created mods that featured more realistic combat, while other mods pitted the player against huge demons that had to be killed without the use of weapons at all.

Despite the positive player response to Id's approach to modding, their move was one that went against the entire culture of the videogame industry. Since the early days of Atari, the videogame industry had jealously guarded their intellectual property through copyrights, patents and secrecy. John Carmack, on the other hand, was a strong believer in the hacker ethic that had motivated Steve Russell and the early hackers at MIT. He was adamantly opposed to the idea of anyone attempting to patent his code (Kushner, 2003, pg 205). Id's later games, the revolutionary *Quake* series, would maintain this position of openness. Eventually, they would take it one step further, releasing both the *Doom* and *Quake* engines as open-source.

Among those to benefit from Id's willingness to share their game engines were the founders of Valve. Created by former Microsoft employees Gabe Newell and Mike Harrington, Valve hired many of its first employees from the Quake modding community (Valve, 2004, pg 7). Their first game, *Half-Life*, was built upon a modified version of the *Quake II* engine that they had licensed from Id. Valve followed Id's lead by making modding a major focus of the game. As a result, *Half-Life* quickly developed a prolific modder community.

Among the many mods created for *Half-Life* was *Counter-Strike*, considered by many to be the most successful mod ever created (Kücklich, 2005). When the mod began to surpass some of Valve's own games in terms of players, they hired on the two creators of the mod so that they could work on their project full time (Valve, 2004, pg 53). When Valve created their Source engine, the next iteration of their *Quake*-based game engine, they designed it to be highly modular, facilitating modders by making the modding process easier, as well as giving them greater control. They also created *Steam,* a digital distribution service that facilitates the sale of games, as well as the distribution of both mods and modding tools. This has led to a very large and active developer community (Trenholme and Smith, 2008).

Most major PC game engines now support modding, each one with unique attributes and associated communities. In addition to the Source engine, popular engines for modding include the CryENGINE, the id Tech 4 engine, and the Unreal engine (Trenholme & Smith, 2008).

The Videogame Industry

From their humble beginnings in the latter half of the twentieth century, videogames have grown to become a multi-billion dollar industry (ESA, 2011). Modern console titles often require the work of hundreds of developers with budgets that have skyrocketed, reaching a hundred million dollars for a single game (Cavalli, 2008). In this climate of blockbuster releases and cutthroat competition, a handful of aspiring programmers tinkering with their favorite game might seem fairly insignificant. So why is modding such a big deal?

Despite its financial success, the videogame industry is not without its problems. The industry can be viewed as a large socio-technical system – a complex network of people, technology and ideas (Hughes, 1987, pg 51). In the creation of any such system, there is a flow of power toward certain groups and away from others. During this process, certain groups become privileged while others are marginalized. This process of privileging and marginalizing is not despotic in nature, but hegemonic (O'Donnell, 2008, pg 86). In other words, there is no authority telling us what games should be made and which groups matter. These concepts about what games should be like simply become "commonsense" understanding about games, and people stop questioning why videogame culture is a certain way (G. King and Krzywinska, 2006, pg 188). These changes are often imperceptible, occurring so gradually that most people don't realize that they happened at all.

In the early days of videogames, the industry (if it could be called an industry) was an incredibly diverse place. Nolan Bushnell, the founder of Atari, set up a makeshift arcade factory in an old roller-rink (Kent, 2001, pg 51). Ralph Baer created the first home videogame system while working for a military contracting company (Halter, 2006, pg 83). Richard Garriott and Roberta Williams, who would go on to found Origin Systems and Sierra On-Line, respectively, both got their start selling their games in Ziploc bags (B. King and Borland, 2003, pg 38; Kushner, 2003, pg 12). As a medium, videogames were still loosely defined, so game developers were free to experiment with new ideas and with new forms of gameplay.

Over the course of the last four decades, the game industry transformed from a handful of independent studios to the sprawling multinational organizations that exist today. Through this transformation, videogames gained better graphics, faster machines and bigger audiences. These changes, however, came at a cost. As budgets increased, so did the need for increased returns, making the industry more and more risk-averse. Today, nearly all major releases are sequels or film adaptations (Deuze, Martin and Allen, 2007, pg 337). Publishers are rarely willing to risk financing new intellectual property, or IP, let alone anything that is drastically new. Instead, they leave the risk to independent developers, taking over only after the game is successful (O'Donnell, 2008, pg 160).

The lack of innovation and creativity within the videogame industry has become a major concern for many game developers, who see their creative expression being stifled and their livelihoods being threatened (Designer X et al, 2000; Davis, 2005). Not surprisingly, it is also a concern for players, who are faced with an increasingly narrow selection of games being produced. With a focus on producing hits, most big-budget games are directed at "hardcore" players (O'Donnell, 2008, pg 160). In essence, this means that the vast majority of games are being directed at young, white males (John, 2006; Kubik, 2010, pg 59). Other groups are marginalized, with their preferences and opinions ignored by game makers.

One way that we can begin to address these growing problems is through the use of modding. Modding lowers the barrier of entry for game development, allowing those who would not normally be able to create a game to do so (Sief El-Nasr and Smith, 2006). Since mods are generally based off modern commercial games, there is often little difference between the quality of mods and other games on the market. In essence, modding allows people to make the games that the industry isn't making.

The Joy of Modding

There are a number of potential benefits associated with modding. Perhaps the most apparent of these is the sheer volume of additional content that mods can add to games. This is also one of the primary motivations for developers to release development kits. By creating additional content beyond that which ships with the game initially, the life of the game is increased, keeping players active and generating attention and prestige for developers (Postigo, 2007, pg 302). Perhaps the best example of this phenomenon is *Doom*. Released in 1994, *Doom*'s easy to modify WAD format spawned a huge modding community. In a time when most consoles don't have a lifespan much longer than five years (Hillis, 2007), *Doom* still maintains an active modding community, which still bestows the coveted "Cacowards" on the best mods of the year (Doomworld, 2010).

While this added content is clearly beneficial to the developers of the original game, perhaps its biggest advantage is that for them, this content is being created free of charge. For the most part, mods are fan-created and distributed over the Internet at no charge to the original developers, nor to the end-user (above the cost of purchasing the original game). Were the developers to generate this volume of content themselves using payed employees, the resulting costs would be substantial. Although it is impossible to place a dollar amount on work being done by untrained hobbyists, Hector Postigo (2007), who has done extensive research on mods and the modding community, estimates that the cost of this additional content could be as high as 50 percent of the total development budget of the original game (pg 303). Thus, modding becomes not only an answer to the players' concerns about new content, but an answer to developers' concerns about rising budgets.

Modders certainly have the ability to cheaply do things that large development studios already do. Perhaps more significant, however, is the fact that modders can do some things that large studios are unable to do. Since the development of a mod is usually not a commercial venture on the part of the modders, they are free to take risks that a large company would be unwilling or unable to take. Mods can create content targeted at small groups of consumers that would be unprofitable for the original development studio to target directly, thus pulling them into the fold as well (Postigo, 2007, pg 311). Successful mods even have the potential to be turned into future commercial titles by the developers, as in the aforementioned case of *Half-Life* and *Counter-Strike*. Not only did Valve not have to expend the resources necessary to create *Counter-Strike* in the first place, upon hiring the modders as full-time employees, they suddenly had a popular game with an established fan-base before the commercial version was even released. In this sense, the modding community serves as a low-stakes testing ground for new ideas that could prove profitable in the future (Jenkins, 2006, pg 163).

The development of mods for existing games can be seen as a counter-hegemonic force that is opening up new avenues for creative expression. Indeed, some mods have created meaningful content for groups that fall outside the videogame industry's narrow target audience. A prime example noted by Postigo is the "FinnWars" mod for the game *Battlefield 1942*, a first-person shooter set in World War II (Postigo, 2007, pg 309). "FinnWars" places the game in the middle of the Finnish Wars, a series of wars in which Finland fought against both the Soviet Union and Nazi Germany in order to maintain its independence (ModDB, 2006). Though culturally significant to the Finnish people, the relative obscurity of these wars outside of Finland makes such a game an unlikely choice for a large development studio. The "FinnWars" mod thus became a way to provide content to a group that could otherwise have gone underserved. Following the success of "FinnWars," the modders were able to form their own independent studio, which is currently developing *FinnWars 2*, a standalone commercial sequel to their original mod (Iceflake Studios, 2010)

Figure 4: The "FinnWars" mod for *Battlefield 1942* created a game that was culturally significant to the Finnish people, despite having an audience that was too narrow for the mainstream videogame industry.

The Perils of Modding

While modding is still an exciting and powerful form of participatory culture, it is not without its perils. Within the modding community, the cyberlibertarian notion of finding wealth, power and self-fulfillment in cyberspace (Winner, 1997) is a common theme. When discussing modding, much like the similar phenomenon of "crowdsourcing," both scholars and journalists often focus on the narratives of the success stories, rather than the phenomenon as a whole. In this sense, we often ignore the influence of existing capitalist structures and fail to recognize that those who reap the greatest benefits are not the individuals, but the large corporations (Brabham, 2008, pg 85). Clearly, work is being done, something of value is being created, and all parties involved gain something from the process. The distribution of these gains, however, is far from equitable.

Despite the generally positive sentiment that exists between large studios and the modding community, the relationship between the two groups can be seen as exploitative (Postigo, 2003, pg 597; Brabham, 2008, pg 83). The modders give their labor to the studio, yet receive no compensation in return. The studio, on the other hand, receives a number of rewards – its games remain in the spotlight longer, new groups are drawn to its games, and new ideas are developed for future games. If the economic factors involved in modding are so incredibly one-sided, why do modders freely give their valuable labor? In analyzing modder motivation, Postigo identified three common themes. Modders saw their endeavors as a way to "break in" to the industry, as a form of artistic expression, and as a way to have more fun with their favorite games (Postigo, 2007, pg 309-310).

As college degrees in game programming and design are a relatively new development "breaking in" to the industry is a complex task with many different potential paths (O'Donnell, 2008, pg 55; Deuze, Martin & Allen, 2007, pg 346). Modding is one path that many developers take. Several companies, such as Valve, are well known for hiring new employees from their own modding communities. With the popularity of modding and the growth of the global modding community, however, employment is far from certain. In fact, as large publishers gain more control over the industry and begin outsourcing more jobs, some studios have attempted to cut costs by using free modder labor, rather than paying a professional developer to do the same work (Deuze, Martin & Allen, 2007, pg 344). With ever-increasing competition for jobs in the game industry, the likelihood of a modder "breaking in" begins to resemble the chances of a college football player being recruited by the NFL. At best, modding could be considered an unpaid, informal internship with no set duration and no promises of future employment.

Even those modders who see modding as simply a form of artistic expression often run into unforeseen problems. Unlike artists who work in other media, modders do not own the content they create (Kücklich, 2005). As the underlying framework of the game is created by the studio (as is the case with many of the artistic elements used in mods), they cannot sell it. In fact, they only have as much control over their work as is given them in the licensing agreement with the studio, the EULA. Should new editions of the original game render a mod obsolete or unplayable, the studio is under no obligation to offer any support or compensation for the modders' lost labors.

Another challenge to creative expression comes in the form of the game engines themselves. Although every medium has its own characteristics and constrains, whether it is videogames, television or oil painting, modders tend to see the technological limitations of their craft in much more tangible terms. Depending on the game they are modifying, they may have the power to make significant changes, or they may be forced to make something very similar to the original game. Regardless of the engine, all mods are in some way derivative of the game they modify. In this way, modding's greatest strength, the ability to create a game without programming it from scratch, can also become a significant stumbling block.

Although modders ultimately do not control the intellectual property they create, they are still required to respect the intellectual property rights of others. Modders often come under fire for copyright infringement. Mods such as "Duke it out in Quake," a mod of *Quake 3* that incorporated elements of Apogee's *Duke Nukem* franchise, and the "GI Joe" mod for *Battlefield 1942* were halted due to copyright issues (Postigo, 2008, pg 61; Nieborg, 2005). Though the modders themselves work without economic incentive, the games that they modify are commercial products. The complex balance between free labor and corporate interests that exists in the mod scene rarely tips in favor of the modders.

Why We Mod

Perhaps more than any other group of videogame creators, modders find themselves between a rock and a hard place. They are not granted the respect and creative freedom granted to full-fledged developers, yet are subject to restrictions that one would not normally expect for unpaid amateur labor. They create works of tremendous value, yet rarely receive any form of compensation. If so many of the legal and economic factors related to modding tend to work against modders, why does anyone bother making mods in the first place?

Though the realities of modding may crush some people's cyberlibertarian dreams of wealth and fame through technology, it doesn't negate the fact that modding is still fun. As Postigo notes, the act of modding allows players to identify more with their games and enjoy them more (Postigo, 2007, pg 309). For those modders, the act of modding itself is justification for the labor it requires. Having worked on several mods myself (and clearly not making it big), I can attest to this fact. It's not a bad way to spend a weekend.

Of course, the fact that modders mod for fun doesn't make the industry's commodification of their leisure time less problematic (Kücklich, 2005). On the contrary, the time that modders devote to working on mods should be taken seriously. In the current climate of videogame culture, modders are very important. Many scholars, such as Sue Morris (2003), have described certain games as "co-creative" media, in which "neither developers nor player-creators can be solely responsible for production of the final assemblage regarded as 'the game.' "

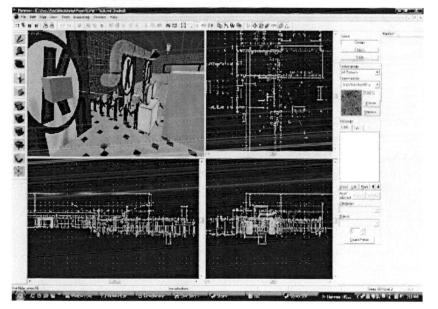

Figure 5: The Valve Hammer Editor, part of the Source SDK allows modders to create their own custom levels for games like *Half-Life 2.*

For aspiring modders, there are a few things to keep in mind. First, that their work is valuable. Although their contributions are often downplayed as being mere hobbies or recreation (Kücklich, 2005), modding creates a great deal of value for both players, who get new content, and for developers, who sell more copies of the original game. In addition to economic value, mods have a great deal of cultural value. In addition to the many videogames that mods have influenced, new forms of expression, such as machinima, or films made using game engines, have come about thanks to modding. Though most machinima is still tightly linked with videogame fan culture, many machinima artists are taking the new medium in new directions (Schott, 2011, pg 119).

Second, modders should always be aware of their rights. While EULAs are designed to protect the interests of the developers, accepting this agreement is a two-way deal. The EULAs that modders must agree to can be considered to be a kind of work contract (Deuze, Martin & Allen, 2007, pg 340). Just as professional game developers must stand up for their rights against exploitative work practices, modders must be willing to do the same (O'Donnell, 2008, pg 275). Although these licensing agreements are restrictive, understanding them can help modders avoid many legal problems. Modders should also make themselves aware of broader laws concerning copyright, fair use, and intellectual property and be willing to stand up against corporations that would try to tell them that these rights do not apply to them.

Finally, modders should understand that the modding community has a great deal of influence. Indeed, some scholars point to fan practices, such as modding, as having the potential to destabilize the current system of mass cultural production (D. Johnson, 2009, pg 54; Jenkins, 2006, pg 135-137). As the modding community grows, the more it will be able to shift the balance of power to tip in its favor. As modders become aware of how much the videogame industry benefits from their labor, it will become more difficult for the industry to deny them their rights as creators and acknowledgment for their work (Kücklich, 2005).

Already, there are several examples of developers giving more rights to modders. In 2003, Linden Labs, the creators of the alternate reality game *Second Life*, changed the terms of their EULA, granting content creators ownership of their work, as well as greater ability to profit from it (Kücklich, 2005). As the buying and selling of user created content is one of the major activities perfomed in *Second Life*, subjecting this content to the usual restrictive licensing agreements would have had a significant effect upon players' overall experience. Linden Labs' relaxing of their IP policies benefited players by allowing for more meaningful and profitable play, which in turn contributed to the popularity of the game.

Such consessions can also occur with IP holders. While developing the game *Star Wars: Battlefront,* LucasArts was faced with a *Battlefield 1942* mod known as "Battlefield Galactic Conquest," a *Star Wars* themed mod that used many of the characters, vehicles and even music from the films. Although they had clear claim on the IP being used, LucasArts chose to allow the mod to continue, perhaps to test the waters before their own game was released (Nieborg, 2005). Despite possible competition from the free mod, *Star Wars: Battlefront* went on to be a commercial success, prompting a sequel and several spin-off games.

As mentioned before, modding is a form of tinkering. Lawrence Lessig (2003) emphasizes the importance of protecting our "freedom to tinker" (pg 8), the ability to reinterpret, to learn from, and to improve technology. The more players exercise that freedom, the more game makers will take it into consideration. As mod support is often one of the first things cut from a game (Deuze, Martin & Allen, 2007, pg 344) or is deliberately removed to give studios greater control (Francis, 2011), it is imperative that modders make their voices heard. Since modders generally represent the most dedicated portion of a game's user base, it is in the best interests of developers to take their concerns seriously. When licensing terms are designed to protect the interests of both developers and modders, both parties benefit from the agreement.

Today is a great day to start modding.

Works Cited

Brabham, D. (2008). Crowdsourcing as a Model for Problem Solving. *Convergence,* 14:1.

Cavalli, E. (2008). GTAIV Budget Tops Gaming Records. *Wired.* Online. Retrieved August 1, 2011 from http://www.wired.com/gamelife/2008/05/creation-of-gta

Davis, G. (2005). GDC Rant Heard 'round the World. *Gamespot.* Online. Retrieved August 1, 2011 from http://www.gamespot.com/news/6120449/gdc-rant-heard-round-the-world

Designer X (alias Costikyan, Greg) et al. (2000). Scratchware Manifesto. Online. Retrieved October August 1, 2011 from: http://www.the-underdogs.info/scratch.php

Deuze, M., Martin C. and Allen, C. (2007). The Professional Identity of Gameworkers. *Convergence* 13:4.

Doomworld. (2010). The 17th Annual Cacowards. Online. Retrieved August 4, 2011 from http://www.doomworld.com/17years/

ESA . (2011). 2011 Essential Facts About the Computer and Video Game Industry. Online. Retrieved July 30, 2011 from http://www.theesa.com/facts/pdfs/ESA_EF_2011.pdf

Francis, T. (2011). Diablo 3 mods "expressly prohibited" by Blizzard. *PC Gamer*. Online. Retrieved August 5, 2011 from http://www.pcgamer.com/2011/08/01/diablo-3-mods-expressly-prohibited-by-blizzard/

Halter, E. (2006). *From Sun Tzu to Xbox: War and Video Games*. New York: Thunder's Mouth Press.

Hillis, S. (2007). Microsoft Sees Long-Life Potential for Xbox 360. *Reuters*. Online. Retrieved August 4, 2011 from http://uk.reuters.com/article/2007/11/06/tech-microsoft-xbox-dc-idUKN0640903820071106

Hughes, T. (1987). The Evolution of Large Technological Systems. In W. Bijker, T. Hughes and T Pinch (Eds.), *The Social Construction of Technological Systems: New Directions in the Sociology and History of Technology* (51-82). Cambridge, Massachusetts: MIT Press.

Iceflake Studios. (2010). The Official FinnWars 2 Homepage. Online. Retrieved August 4, 2011 from http://iceflakestudios.com/fw2static/

Jenkins, H. (2006). *Convergence Culture: Where Old and New Media* Collide. New York: New York University Press.

John, S. (2006). Un/Realistically Embodied: The gender conceptions of realistic game design. *Advanced Visual Interfaces AVI, Workshop on Gender & Interaction, Real & virtual women in a male world*. Venice, Italy.

Johnson, A. (1996). 'Official' Castle Smurfenstein Home Page. Online. Retrieved June 27, 2011 from http://evlweb.eecs.uic.edu/aej/smurf.html

Johnson, D. (2009). StarCraft Fan Craft: Game Mods, Ownership, and Totally Incomplete Conversions. *The Velvet Light Trap*, 64.

Kent, S. (2001). *The Ultimate History of Videogames.* London: Three Rivers Press.

King, B. and Borland, J. (2003). *Dungeons and Dreamers: The Rise of Computer Game Culture from Geek to Chic.* Emeryville, California: McGraw-Hill.

King, G. and Krzywinska, T. (2006). *Tomb raiders & space invaders: Videogame forms & contexts.* London: I.B. Tauris.

Kubik, E. (2010). *From Girlfriend To Gamer: Negotiating Place In The Hardcore/Casual Divide Of Online Video Game Communities.* Bowling Green State University.

Kücklich, J. (2005). Precarious Playbour. Modders and the Digital Games Industry. *The Fibreculture Journal*, 5.

Kushner, D. (2003). *Masters of Doom: How Two Guys Created an Empire and Transformed Pop Culture.* New York: Random House.

Lessig, L. (2005). Creative commons. Paper presented at the 2005 Annual ITU Conference, "Creative Dialogues." Oslo,Network for IT-Research and Competence in Education (ITU), University of Oslo.

Levy, S. (1984). *Hackers: Heroes of the Computer Revolution.* New York: Dell Publishing.

Miller, R. (2008). Ask Joystiq: Chex Quest, He-Man and Broken 360 Gamepads. *Joystiq.* Online. Retrieved June 24, 2011 from http://www.joystiq.com/2008/04/18/ask-joystiq-chex-quest-he-man-and-broken-360-gamepads/

ModDB. (2006). Finnwars. Online. Retrieved August 4, 2011 from http://www.moddb.com/mods/ finnwars

Morris, S. (2003). WADs, Bots and Mods: Multiplayer FPS Games as Co-Creative Media. *Level Up: Digital Games Research Conference*. M. Copier & J. Raessens (Eds.). Utrecht, Netherlands.

Nevins, P. (1999). Dead Smurf Software. Online. Retrieved June 27, 2011 from http://cvnweb.bai.ne.jp/~preston//other/deadsmurf/index.html

Nieborg, D. (2005). Am I Mod or Not? — An Analysis of First Person Shooter Modification Culture. *Creative Gamers Seminar — Exploring Participatory Culture in Gaming*. Tampere, Finland.

O'Donnell, C. (2008). *The Work/Play of the Interactive New Economy: Video Game Development in the United States and India*. Rensselaer Polytechnic Institute.

Postigo, H. (2003). From Pong to Planet Quake: Post-Industrial Transitions from Leisure to Work. *Information, Communication & Society*, 6:4.

Postigo, H. (2007). Of Mods and Modders: Chasing Down the Value of Fan-Based Digital Game Modification. *Games and Culture*, 2.

Postigo, H. (2008). Video Game Appropriation through Modification: Attitudes Concerning Intellectual Property among Modders and Fans. *Convergence: The International Journal of Research into New Media Technologies*, 14.

Promotion Marketing Association. (2005). 1998 Reggie Gold Winners. Online. Retrieved June 24, 2011 from http://web.archive.org/web/20050220030617/http://pmalink.org/members/reggies/1998_reggie_winners2.asp

Schott, G. (2011). The Production of Machinima: A Dialogue between Ethnography,Culture and Space. *International Journal of Business, Humanities and Technology*, 1:1.

Seif El-Nasr, M. & Smith, B. (2006). Learning Through Game Modding. *ACM Computers in Entertainment*, 4:1.

Sloane, M. (1997, August 13) Cereal Offer Provides Good Fun. *The Vindicator*. Pg C2. Available Online at http://news.google.com/newspapers?nid=jtusTj6o6osC&dat=19970813&printsec=frontpage&hl=en

Trenholme, D and Smith, S. (2008). Computer game engines for developing first-person virtual environments. *Virtual Reality,* 12.

Turner, F. (2006). *From Counterculture to Cyberculture: Stewart Brand, the Whole Earth Network, and the Rise of Digital Utopianism.* Chicago: University of Chicago Press.

Valve. (2004). *Half Life 2: Raising the Bar.* Roseville, California: Prima Games.

Warner, S. (1981). *Castle Wolfenstein* [Videogame]. Monrovia, Maryland: Muse Software.

Chapter 2

Between

Fact and Fiction

in Cultural Heritage

51

Natalie M. Underberg

52

Between Fact and Fiction in Cultural Heritage

Natalie M. Underberg, University of Central Florida,
4000 Central Florida Parkway, Orlando, FL 32816,
Natalie.Underberg@ucf.edu

In this chapter I discuss my work on an educationsl computer game mod designed to teach about Depression-era Ybor City, Florida history and culture titled the *Turkey Maiden Educational Computer Game* (Underberg, 2008). The area is known for its historic cigar industry and Latin immigration population. The game itself is based on a Spanish folktale collected from Ybor City, Florida and was adapted into a video game mod using the popular Role Playing Game (RPG) *Neverwinter Nights*.

Introduction to the Project: Game Mod Production and Design with Neverwinter Nights

The creation of the *Neverwinter Nights* mod required building and managing a team of students under the direction of myself and with the valuable assistance of lead programmer Chantale Fontaine (a former UCF student). Independent study classes were arranged with primarily undergraduate Digital Media students with experience in the following areas: portrait illustration (capable of producing somewhat realistic portraits for video game characters); writing (creative writers with role-playing game experience to develop conversations and side-quests); 3D art and animation (students experienced with 3D texture creation, character modeling, and character rigging); programming (programmers with experience writing and compiling modules and writing scripts for them—knowledge of the *Neverwinter Nights* toolset was a significant plus in this area); and music (students with music and sound effects composition experience). In addition, students conducted periodic beta-testing to make sure the game was playable as it was being developed.

To organize and be able to draw from the historical materials, as well as to enable students as they joined the team to familiarize themselves with both content and technical materials related to the project, relevant documents were made available through a project Yahoo Group according to several categories: information specific to our game, keys needed to install the game, images and resources related to historical Ybor City, the custom content creation guide made available by the creators of *Neverwinter Nights*, and links to Websites with other resources needed to build the game such as tutorials.

This content management organization facilitated both project development and management with current team members, and greatly increased our ability to quickly get new team members up-to-speed and working on the project. For example, we could direct a student who wanted to create 2D character portraits for a class project to a "Character Portrait Wish List" under the "Database" section of the Yahoo Groups to see a list of the portraits needed.

Because of the amount of historical materials involved in developing the game design, we needed to first sort some of the scanned images into the relevant categories before 2D and 3D models could be created. Students were asked to crop with image and caption only the images in these subfolders so they are separate pictures, and to organize them by putting into the different "photo albums" in the Yahoo Group site (making new folders as necessary). To make this process easier, the scans were uploaded as zip files.

Developing the 3D models involved 3 students working approximately 3 hours per week each during one semester. A list of tutorials on in the "Vault" was available at http://nevault.ign.com/modules/ tutorials/viewlets, and students were directed in particular to the toolset section. In particular, students were directed to view and follow the "viewlets" on "Toolset Lessons" and "Scripting Lessons" (available at http://nwvault.ign.com/?dir=resources/ tutorials/viewlets). Other resources the students found helpful included Bioware's toolset introduction (http://nwn.bioware.com/builders/toolsetintro. html), the Script Generator (particularly helpful if students do not want to have to write scripts from scratch) (http://nwvault.ign.com/View. php?view=other.Detail&id=625), and the Gestalt's System (for creating cutscenes) (http://nwvault.ign.com/View.php?view=other.Detail&id=2570).

Modeling tasks involved creating clothing (male suit, traditional dance dress, special occasion dress); buildings (the mutual aid society Centro Asturiano, the cigar factory, the cigar worker's house, and, later, the home of the cigar factory owner); and animals (the turkey). In addition to viewing and using tutorials on how to create new models, students also imported existing files and modified them (using the import and export tool "nwmax").

To develop the 3D models for clothing, for example, lead programmer Chantale Fontaine first uploaded sample mdls and plts to the Yahoo Group for the student team members to examine. She also directed students to the relevant subheading in the resources section on "PLT" for the students to learn about how to edit PLTs (which required some understanding of the format and certain tools).

Creating dresses for the women avatars proved easier than creating realistic-looking suits for the male characters. Fontaine at first tried to put together the image of a suit using a modern clothing "hak", and then mixed and matched a few more pieces of men's clothes to see if she could better approximate the men's clothing of the era using the a modern men's clothes "hak." As these images were developed, they were posted in the game screenshots album section of the Yahoo Group for the team to view.

The texturing work, though less of a priority, was still necessary in the game production process. To facilitate the creation of an appropriate "look" for the buildings in the game space (changing them from "gothic" to early 20th century U.S.), the students re-textured 6 very slightly different sets of walls, floors and ceilings. To prevent students from becoming confused, Fontaine divided the 7 sets into 7 folders name by the terrain name (e.g., Study, Living1, etc.). Within each folder students could find the set-specific files. To enable easier browsing of the models, Fontaine put /NWNMdlView.exe/ in each set folder. The textures themselves were placed in a separate folder ("textures"), so that students could move the contents (DDS) of the textures folder to the set they were working on at the time. Certain textures gave the game production team problems. For example, the factory texture took a good deal of work to re-do. Both gmax and chiliskinner were initially used, but to no avail, until Fontaine found a video with directions for re-doing textures using chiliskinner (available at http://nwvault.ign.com/View.php?view =movies.Detail&id=187).

Actually scripting a digital cultural heritage game using a commercial role-playing game engine provided its own challenges, as those familiar with *Neverwinter Nights* can probably imagine. As Fontaine was scripting the first task, she found that she had to spend considerable time trying to prevent the father character in the game from being able to kill Rosa (the main character), as this capacity and tendency is built into the game engine. Seeing the father keep hitting Rosa over the head with the book she's supposed to be reading makes clear the underlying potential for violence woven deep into the game logic of the original work; a factor that has to be taken into account when developing an educational game for public school students.

Designing and Using Game Mods for Cultural Heritage Education

Designing cultural heritage educational computer games, of course, requires creatively grappling with the expressive potential of the digital medium. Adapting a tale to a new medium, in particular, means understanding how the medium itself would influence the entire project. This required

55

attempting to determine the "spirit" of the story and how best to use the potential of new media to visualize the core elements of the tale.

In her article, "Literary Film Adaptation and the Form/Content Dilemma," Elliott (2004), examines the issue of form vs. content through various models of adaptation that have been applied to Emily Bronte's *Wuthering Heights*. How a story created in one medium (literature) is adapted to another medium (film) can reveal insights into the nature of storytelling from form to form. Elliott's essay outlines several models, which volume editor Ryan succinctly summarizes here:

> "The 'psychic model' tells, for instance, that a novel's spirit can migrate into a new body; it is therefore the film's mission to capture this wandering spirit. The 'ventriloquist model' empties the body of the novel of its spiritual content and gives it a new voice. The 'genetic model' postulates a common genetic code, or narrative, deep structure, shared by the bodies of two siblings. The 'merging model' has two spirits reuniting, as the bodies decompose, and the appreciator sees the adaptation as the sum of novel and film. The 'incarnational model' regards the film as the visible body to which the novel's abstract language aspires. The 'trumping model,' finally, sees the film as performing the equivalent of a sex-change operation: the spirit of the novel grew in the wrong body, and the film restores it to its rightful material support" (Ryan, 2004: 198-199).

In the "psychic" model, the text has a "spirit" with which the audience has a kind of psychic connection. The spirit is elusive, so adaptation must capture the spirit to communicate it via changing mediums. In this model, one begins with authorial intent, imagination, or personality and ends with what lingers in the minds of the audience after experiencing the story. Being true to the" spirit" of the text means having to be unfaithful to its letter or form; in other words, it cannot be too literal an adaptation. "Authorial intent" can be used to validate contemporary points of view or value systems (Elliott in Ryan, 2004).

Arguably, the "spirit" of "The Turkey Maiden" is a female Spanish variant of a European *märchen* or fairy tale in which a plucky heroine undergoes a series of quests to emerge successful at the end—and win her "prince." Remaining faithful to its "spirit" in a changing form—a computer game—meant making changes to the story to integrate specific quests and puzzles related to Ybor

City history and culture. This is consistent with the "sprit" of the story because the heroine takes matters into her own hands in the folktale and does what is necessary to succeed in her adventure.

In addition to the "psychic" model, a closer consideration of the "genetic" and "incarnational" models can help explain the digital adaptation of "The Turkey Maiden." In the genetic model, there is a common genetic code, or narrative deep structure, shared by the two stories. This model, based in narratology, equates "deep" narrative structure with genetic structure, and it is that which transfers between literature and film (awaiting a kind of "body"). The narrative, in the sense of a series of events, can transfer from novel to film, but with different plot techniques like sequencing. In the "incarnational" model, the film is the body which gives visual form to the novel's abstract language. In this view, the word is only partially expressive, and needs to be incarnated in order to be fully expressed. In this process, the signs become less abstract. The film becomes the fulfillment of what was only described in the novel—and makes what was only described specific in ways not always possible by use of language alone (Elliott in Ryan, 2004). Together, these models offer ways to view the decisions behind the design and creation of the project.

In "The Turkey Maiden," the same narrative deep structure was maintained between published tale and computer game: the story is a typical *märchen* that can be broken down into functions (Vladimir Propp 1968), and is essentially a hero's tale. Sharon Sherman (1997) notes that video games frequently are based on elements of the hero's journey, incorporating elements of Propp's functions and the hero cycle outlined by Jung and Campbell (1997). Sherman (1997) and I (Underberg 2005) each point out that the European *märchen* is really an elaboration on the middle part of the hero cycle focusing on adventures. While its basic identity as a Cinderella-type story (in the sense of sharing similarities with the well-known Aarne-Thompson tale type 510) is reproduced, however, visualization makes possible storytelling techniques like repetition present in the written tale to be maintained—but visually and through action. For example, Rosa's mistreatment by her stepmother and stepsisters is enacted in the actions of the Non-Player Characters (NPCs) who harass Rosa and make her perform chores—and they will not let her alone until she completes them.

Similarly, the Centro Asturiano (a Spanish mutual aid society in Ybor City) is really a place, yet it functions as much narratively as factually in the game. This is because it serves as a physical representation of the Rosa character's desire for food and warmth and by extension, safety. So the fictional or fantasy element of the dwarf character being able to provide food and warmth changes to the Centro Asturiano's ability to provide the same as a mutual aid society. Instead of providing her with food and warmth directly, the dwarf brings her to the Centro (after she completes a task) where she can encounter food and the warmth of people feasting and dancing all around her. This resonates with Glassberg's (1996) argument that: "Public historians can participate in the process of placemaking and contribute to local residents' sense of place by adding a sense of location to local residents' sense of emotional attachment, helping residents and visitors alike to see what ordinarily cannot be seen: both the memories attracted to places and the larger social and economic processes that shaped how the places were made" (Glassberg, 1996: 21). Creating these digital cultural heritage environments, however, involves balancing the need to create an intriguing illusion into which the audience will be immersed, and successfully delivering accurate cultural information and conveying fact-based lessons (Kenderdine in Cameron and Kenderdine, 2007).

"The Turkey Maiden" as educational computer game mod differs from its source material in several ways, but most obviously in two: the setting was changed from the generic fairy tale world of kings and queens in "a land far, far away" to the specific setting from which the tale was collected:

Depression-era Ybor City, Florida, and quests were introduced specific to Ybor City history and culture in order to teach about the Florida city. These changes required grappling with balancing the fantasy content of the story with its concrete historical setting. Specifically, the changes involved finding ways to appropriately present Ybor City's history as the former "cigar capital of the world" to a primary and secondary public school audience.

The transition of traditional tales, particularly the European märchen or magic tale, to literature (and later, film) has been the subject of numerous studies, including multiple texts by Jack Zipes (see, for example, *Breaking the Magic Spell: Radical Theories of Folk and Fairy Tales*, 1990, and *Fairy Tales and the Art of Subversion*, 2006), and other studies which analyze the literary adaptation process of the well-known (and frequent literary and film source) Brothers Grimm's tales in particular (Ruth Bottigheimer's Grimms' *Bad Girls and Bold Boys*, 1987 and Maria Tatar's *The Hard Facts of the Grimms' Fairy Tales*, 2003 are two such examples). As the titles of Bottigheimer's and Tatar's books suggest, gender is an important concern when considering the literary adaptation process, and, indeed, emerged as one of the main issues with which the game mod project had to grapple.

Gender representation in computer games and in computer game playing has been the subject of a significant amount of scholarship. One focus of studies examines gender differences in computer socialization and use, finding that boys more often receive computers as gifts and encouragement to use them, more frequently play computer games, and more often dominate computer use in the classroom (see, for example, Bullen and Kenway in Yelland and Rubin, 2002). Another focus of scholarship is the representation of females in computer games themselves. These studies point out that women are generally included in games as largely helpless or overtly sexualized characters (see, for example, Littleton and Hoyles in Hayward and Wollen, 1993).

In her study of computer games and folklore, Sharon Sherman (1997) argues that many commercial games' reliance on the hero's journey narrative both ensures the games' popular appeal and contributes to gender stereotyping (Sherman, 1997). In contrast, "The Turkey Maiden" computer game mod seeks to subvert gender stereotypes precisely because it is based on folklore. As a tale collected by Ralph Steele Boggs (actually Tale Type 511, but very similar to the much more well-known folktale "Cinderella"), it closely resembles variants of Cinderella collected from female Spanish narrators (see Taggart, 1990).

Central to these variants is the self-sufficient and "take-charge" nature of the Cinderella character—it is she who takes the initiative to seek work at the palace, and she who takes the actions necessary to open her nuts and don the dresses when necessary to save herself, and, ultimately, the prince. Rosa has help, certainly, in the form of a magical dwarf and turkeys—much like the fairy Godmother of the more commonly known literary and, later, film versions. However, as Kay Stone pointed out years ago in her article "Things Walt Disney Never Told Us" (1986), heroines of oral tales are capable of solving their own problems when necessary (see also Yolen in Dundes, 1986). Rosa's active character is further amplified in the computer game adaptation because of the quests she must successfully complete throughout in order to advance in the game. For example, before receiving the gift of three nuts from her father (from which the dresses will eventually come) she must first find and tell to her father (a lector, or reader in the cigar factory) a particular story involving the Spanish folklore character Quevedo so he can read it to the workers tomorrow (and hence stave off replacement by the new medium of the radio). Rosa must use her wits, and her plucky spirit, throughout the adventure.

Figure 1; Rosa from the *Turkey Maiden Educational Computer Game* Courtesy: Natalie M. Underberg.

A second challenge faced by the game design team was finding appropriate ways to present potentially controversial subject matter. Because "The Turkey Maiden" is an educational computer game yet set in Ybor City, Florida, (arguably best known for the cigar industry that flourished there), I had to confront the issue of how to present a controversial topic (tobacco smoking) in a public school setting (intended for 8th and 9th graders). The potentially troublesome nature of the topic is increased by the heightened capacity for realism made possible by the computer game medium. Tang and Tan (in King and Krzywinska, 2002) point out that computer game storytelling has more of a visual than a literary narrative structure.

It is the increased realism and potential for interactivity that makes the game storytelling experience unique. Games utilize filmic techniques but without the editing that characterizes movie narration—in its place the player interacts with an elaborately simulated 3D environment. The Digital Media students at UCF created 3D models of Ybor City structures such as the cigar factory (the "palace" in the game) and the Centro Asturiano (a Spanish mutual aid society). They also created clothing for the avatars (appropriate for Depression-era Tampa, Florida), and designed the interior of buildings to hold objects and avatars reminiscent of the time and place. These elements of realism aided the cause of utilizing the computer game mod to teach students about Florida history and culture. To this end, the fantasy fairy tale world mentioned but not described in any real detail in the story collected by Boggs was instead filled with Ybor City analogues: the king was changed to Señor Rey (owner of El Rey cigar factory), the prince was then referred to as "*el hijo del Rey*" (the son of Rey, or "the son of the king" in Spanish), the palace becomes the factory and environs, and so on.

Figure 2; Screen shot of the cigar factory exterior in the *Turkey Maiden Educational Computer Game.*   Courtesy: Natalie M. Underberg.

For this project, the game design and production team attempted to present the topic of tobacco in an age- and school environment-appropriate way in the game. The team accomplished this by integrating the facts surrounding the cigar industry into the computer game story, and presenting cigar factory workers in multiple roles. By playing the game, and through navigating the basic structure of having to successfully receive and open the three nuts to reveal magical dresses (which is the basic outline of a "Cinderella" story), the player must accomplish specific tasks. These are:

> 1) correctly identifying a particular Spanish folktale amongst other Spanish folklore to help her father a lector or reader in the cigar factory find the right story to read to the workers;

> 2) helping a female factory worker find the special *vuelta abajo* tobacco leaves she needs to make the top quality cigars for which the area was known (and thereby receive the use of a chaveta, the knife used to cut the leaves to open one of her nuts to escape danger);

> 3) correctly describing a Spanish mutual aid society to a helpful donor figure so she can find food and warmth there;

> 4) interacting with different Spanish dancers to identify the correct one who can lead her to the flowers she needs on her quest; and

> 5) telling the guard the story of Jose Martí (the revolutionary leader) so she can enter the house to cure the "prince."

Thus, the quests in the game are built around topics about which any history or social science lesson plan about Ybor City would likely be built, including the role of the *lector* in the cigar factory, tools and materials used in the cigar industry, the significance of mutual aid societies in immigrant communities, the place of dance in Latin culture, and the connection between Cuban revolutionary leader Jose Martí and Ybor City. It was important for players to be able to see those involved with the tobacco industry in a more complex way. For example, the father was understood primarily as a lector (reader) rather than as a smoker or producer of tobacco products. He is a man of learning as much as anything else. This relates to an implicit lesson of the *Turkey Maiden Educational Computer Game:* the importance of literacy and reading skills for the success of Rosa, and the player/student.

Slater (1987) argues that the subject of history has an important part to play in teaching about controversial subjects in the classroom. Doing so today involves having students critically evaluate sources, putting contemporary events in perspective, and presenting students with potentially contrary viewpoints (1987). Since I realized that certain issues touched on in the game were ones that educators and arts facilitators might want to address in more depth, I included a curriculum packet with the the game which allows students to go into more depth about the history and culture of Ybor City. For example, students can complete activities such as researching the experiences of women cigar factory workers, or exploring the architecture of cigar workers' homes.

62

Conclusion: Results and Lessons Learned

The project was exhibited and presented at several venues, including a workshop for teachers and arts facilitators in collaboration with UCF CREATE, an arts and education consortium. At this event, participants had the opportunity to learn about the game and discuss how it could be integrated into the primary and secondary school curriculum. It was also exhibited at the Florida Digital Media Alliance's "Games for Good" conference in Orlando, and presented at the Society for Applied Anthropology and American Folklore Society conferences. Finally, the project appeared in the Folklife in Education Handbook (revised edition), a resource used by teachers and arts facilitators around the country.

We learned several important lessons from this project. In developing the educational aspects of the game and curriculum, initially the lessons, although interdisciplinary, tended to lean towards social science (history). But in working with local educators and Arts for a Complete Education (A.C.E.), we were able to expand the curriculum into Language Arts and Visual Arts, thus broadening the potential educational applications of the project. Yet, we also found, for practical reason we needed to focus on subjects that were being tested by the state (in the FCAT exam) required of all public schools--and that meant Language Arts and Math. This inspired the team to consider ways to develop a curriculum focused on the video game itself, and incorporating our insights into how the project was created in a way that involves primary and secondary students in an age-appropriate way in the production process. This, we believe, has great potential for further integrating the technology into the classroom.

In addition to creating an educational resource for primary and secondary students, the project also presented an opportunity to involve UCF Digital Media graduate students in an applied project that developed both 3D modeling and research skills. Students in a Directed Research class worked with me and with graduate student Traci Yeager (who tutored the students in 3D modeling) to develop new models for the game in the second phase of development, in an effort to add increased historical accuracy to the game environment and the characters in it. Students learned about the numerous elements that go into making (or modding) a video game. Aside from programming and 3D modeling, they learned, there are a number of other, equally important tasks, especially the research behind the game that is necessary when based on historical materials.

To this end, students were assigned to develop a new model for the game from start to finish--from engaging in historical research about 1930s Ybor City, Florida to ensure the authenticity of the models and content, to learning the basics of 3D modeling in Maya, to learning how to create a static model based on their historical research. They used a combination of library, archive, and on-site research, including a research trip to Ybor City to visit museums and historic sites, talk to people, and take photo documentation to be used for the models in the game. As their final reflective papers revealed, valuable lessons were learned during the process about how to balance the need for authenticity with the realities of video game design and storytelling about cultural heritage. For example, one student investigated how to locate a forest or some sort of open landscape surrounding the Ybor City area where the cigar workers homes would be located. This was necessary to set the Turkey Maiden folktale--in which an important scene takes place in a forest--within the Ybor City setting, and to do so in a way that made sense in terms of the physical and social environment of the city. To do this, she had to discover if and where maps of Ybor City from the 1920s would be located, which involved contacting historical preservation groups, exploring online digital collections, and digitizing archive collections for use in game development. In another project, a student struggled to find the right balance between creating historically realistic 3D models and ensuring that they were not too high in their polygon/vector numbers that they slowed down the game engine. She had to make adaptive decisions about how to strike this balance, finally finding that she needed to leave out door handles and other small additions to the fender that are seen in the original picture reference.

Through exploring one particular case study of a heritage-based *Neverwinter Nights* mod, I have discussed issues surrounding the sometimes productive, sometimes problematic relationship between historical accuracy and enabling an interactive and engaging experience for audiences in a way that creates cultural experiences for players (Roussou 2002). The *Turkey Maiden Educational Computer Game* project proved a valuable test bed for these lessons.

References

Aarne, A. & S. Thompson (1961). *The Types of the Folktale.* Helsinki: Folklore Fellows Communication, n184 (2nd revised edition).

Bottigheimer, R. (1987). *Grimms' Bad Girls and Bold Boys: The Moral and Social Vision of the Tales.* New Haven, CT: Yale University Press.

Bullen, E. & J. Kenway (2002). Who's Afraid of a Mouse? Girls, Information, Technology and Educational Pleasure. In N. Yelland and A. Rubin (Eds.), *Ghosts in the Machine: Women's Voices in Research with Technology* (pp. 54-69). New York: Peter Lang.

Congdon, K. (2001). *Uncle Monday and Other Florida Tales.* Jackson, MS: University Press of Mississippi.

Elliott, K. (2004). Literary Film Adaptation and the Form/Content Dilemma. In M. Ryan (Ed.), *Narrative Across Media: The Languages of Storytelling* (pp. 220-243). Lincoln, NB: University of Nebraska Press.

Glassberg, D. (1996). Public History and the Study of Memory. The Public Historian, 18, 7-23.

Kenderdine, S. (2007). Speaking in Rama. In F. Cameron & S. Kenderdine (Eds.), *Theorizing Digital Cultural Heritage: A Critical Discourse* (pp.301-331). Cambridge, MA: The MIT Press.

Littleton, K. & C. Hoyles (1993). The Gendering of Information Technology. In P. Howard & T. Wollen (Eds.), *Future Visions: Introduction and Development of New Screen Technologies* (pp. 33-54). London: British Film Institute.

Propp, V. (1968). *Morphology of the Folktale*. Austin: University of Texas Press.

Roussou, M. (2002). Virtual Heritage: From the Research Lab to the Broad Public. *Proceedings of the VAST Euroconference*, Arezzo, Italy.

Ryan, M. (2004). Moving Pictures. In M. Ryan (Ed.), *Narrative Across Media: The Languages of Storytelling* (pp. 195-202). Lincoln, NB: University of Nebraska Press.

Sherman, S. (1997). Perils of the Princess: Gender and Genre in Video Games. Western Folklore, 56, 243-58.

Slater, J. (1987). History and Controversy in the Classroom. History Today, 37, 6-7.

Stone, K. (1986). Things Walt Disney Never Told Us. In Claire Farrer (Ed.), Women and Folklore. Long Grove, IL: Waveland Press.

Taggart, J. (1990). *Enchanted Maidens: Gender Relations in Spanish Folktales of Courtship and Marriage*. Princeton, NJ: Princeton University Press.

Tang, W. & M. Tan (2002). Vision and Virtuality: The Construction of Narrative Space in Film and Computer Games. In G. King & T. Krzywinska (Eds.), *Screenplay: Cinema/Videogames/Interfaces*. London: Wallflower Press.

Tatar, M. (2003). *The Hard Facts of the Grimms' Fairy Tales*. Princeton, NJ: Princeton University Press.

Underberg, N. (2008). *The Turkey Maiden Educational Computer Game*. Folklore, 119, 201-217.

Underberg, N. (2005). The Hero Cycle. In. J. Garry and H. El-Shamy (Eds.), *Archetypes and Motifs in Folklore and Literature: A Handbook*. Armonk, NY: M.E. Sharpe.

Yolen, J. (1989). America's Cinderella. In Alan Dundes (Ed.), *Cinderella: A Casebook,* ed. Alan Dundes (pp. 294-308). Madison, WI: University of Wisconsin Press.

Zipes, J. (2006). *Fairy Tales and the Art of Subversion: The Classical Genre for Children and the Process of Civilization*. New York: Routledge.

Zipes, J. (1990). *Breaking the Magic Spell: Radical Theories of Folk and Fairy Tales*. New York: Routledge.

Chapter 3

Use of

"The Elder Scrolls
Construction Set"

to create a

Virtual History Lesson

Eric Fassbender

68

Use of 'The Elder Scrolls Construction Set' to create a virtual history lesson

Eric Fassbender, Charles Darwin University,
Ellengowan Drive, School of Creative Arts and
Humanities, Darwin, NT, 0831, Australia,
eric.fassbender@cdu.edu.au, eric@fassbender.com.au

Introduction

Technological developments and innovations in the past two decades have had an unprecedented impact on society and educational practices. The use of information over the Internet, improvements in graphics performance and human-computer interaction have enabled new forms of interactive teaching. Together, or facilitated by these improvements, in the past 5 to 10 years we have seen a strong interest in what is commonly referred to as serious games. These serious games use videogame technology to communicate real-world issues by combining entertainment and education, and the tools that allow the creation of educational content have become increasingly powerful and user-friendly.

69

One example of such content creation tools are computer game construction sets, which offer us the ability to create astounding interactive virtual worlds at little cost. In this chapter I describe how the construction set of a professional and commercial computer game has been used to create a virtual environment that teaches the history of the Macquarie Lighthouse. This virtual history lesson then served as a framework for experiments on the effect of music on memory in virtual environments. We won't go into the details of these experiments, as this is an entirely different topic; instead, we will focus on the development of the history lesson and the tools that were used to achieve this. Saying that, we will need some of the background information of the virtual history lesson to understand, why a computer game construction set was used for the creation of the virtual environment.

The experimental environment, called VirSchool (*Virtual School*), was aimed to be similar to a real-world scenario in which users would be talking to another person or teacher. For the creation of this environment, I evaluated a number of construction sets and virtual environments with building and scripting capabilities (Torque (2009), Neverwinter Nights (2009), Second Life (2011) to name a few).

While Torque is a very powerful and flexible game engine, it can require a medium level of programming or scripting effort and my experiences in this area are fairly limited. Thus, despite the very powerful graphics engine of Torque, it was unsuitable for my requirements. The next construction set that I evaluated was Neverwinter Nights, which is focused on pseudo-3D games. Such pseudo-3D games are situated in 3D environments, yet the display of these environments is on a flat two-dimensional plane; sometimes these games are called 2.5D (MacGregor, J., & Leung, S., (2009). However, since I wanted to give the teaching environment a more realistic feeling, Neverwinter Nights was not suitable either, and I continued my evaluation with Second Life. While Second Life is a 'true' 3D environment, it requires a permanent connection to the Internet and, like with Torque, programming and scripting knowledge is required to achieve interactivity.

The last construction set that I evaluated was 'The Elder Scrolls Construction Set' (TESCS), version 1.0.303 (Elder Scrolls, 2011). The first thing I noticed was that TESCS offers a first-person camera viewpoint, which was very useful for my purposes as I wanted to achieve a high level of involvement with a first-person viewpoint. Secondly, TESCS offers a sophisticated dialog system, which allows not only the creation of the dialog but also features a built-in lip synchronisation for the Avatar delivering the dialog. Thus, it allows a lot of flexibility in terms of creating a storyline. Most importantly, however, I was able to achieve the functionality that I needed for my study without any programming skills, as TESCS is almost completely a 'point-and-click' construction set. Furthermore, custom 3D models can be imported into TESCS, which was essential for the present study in order to create a model of the Macquarie Lighthouse and surrounds.

In the sections that follow I will describe the import of a custom 3D model into the construction set, landscape creation and character and dialogue creation, including synchronisation of recorded audio with the avatar lip movements. Before going into the technical details of these features, however, it seems adequate to outline the historical background of the Macquarie Lighthouse so that the requirements for building the environment become clearer.

Historical Background

Despite its importance to Australian settlement, the history of the Macquarie Lighthouse in Sydney is not widely known, thus, it was an ideal topic for the evaluation of memory and was used for the experimental framework that was used for the study. Initially, the intention was to create an interactive virtual environment. However, after engaging with the literature on the topic I decided to create a non-interactive virtual environment because it has been shown that interactivity may interfere with the experience of story (Bizzocchi & Woodbury, 2003). Another argument for creating a non-interactive environment was that it provided me with better control of the experimental variables.

The justification for this decision is that interactions that occur within virtual environments and video games can be highly complex; and if interactivity (which is all about exploration, options and choices) had been allowed, it would have been impossible to draw precise conclusions regarding the effect of background music on memory, which was what the study sought to investigate. This problem becomes more obvious if we consider an example of Participant A, who wanders around freely in the virtual environment and interacts with three different Avatars (virtual personas). Where Participant A takes a certain route and order in which he or she receives information from different Avatars, Participant B could (and most likely would) visit these three Avatars in a different order and listen to a different piece of music at the point when the year of construction of the lighthouse (or another historical fact) was conveyed. Not only would there be a problem with the music stimulus that is not played at the same time, but also it could not be guaranteed that the participants would receive the historical information in the correct sequential order. These problems were avoided by creating a computer-animated video that delivered a) the historical information in the same order to each participant and b) played the same music stimulus to the participants at the exact same time at which the historical facts were presented to each participant.

Despite the restrictions of non-interactivity, the history lesson was created as similar as possible to a typical conversation with an Avatar in a full-feature computer-based role-playing game. Development of the VirSchool included research into the historical background of the Macquarie Lighthouse, creation of an accurate 3D model and landscape, creation of the virtual environment, the recording of the Avatar dialogue and the screen capture of the video animations.

The Macquarie Lighthouse (see Figure 1) is Australia's first lighthouse; some even say it was the first lighthouse in the southern hemisphere (Reid, 1988) in (Casey & Lowe, 2005). It is situated on the South Head peninsula of Sydney's Port Jackson harbour entrance and the lighthouse that we are looking at today is the second lighthouse that was built in almost the same spot as the first one. The history of the Macquarie Lighthouse begins with the colonisation of Australia and the arrival of the First Fleet in 1788. According to Casey and Lowe (2005), as early as 1790 a flagstaff was erected near the site where the lighthouse is located today. The flagstaff's original purpose was of course to indicate the harbour entrance to incoming ships but more importantly, to signal the arrival of a particular ship to the colonists who were desperately awaiting supplies from England because they were running short on food.

In the years following the erection of the first flagstaff, the flagstaff was supported by a stone column (1790), upgraded (1792), rebuilt (1797) and extended by a fire beacon (between 1793 and 1805). On the 1st of January 1810 Colonel Lachlan Macquarie started his duty as Governor of New South Wales and in 1818 architect Francis Howard Greenway finished the construction of the first Macquarie Lighthouse. As early as five years after the end of the construction, repairs had to be conducted because parts of the building were falling apart. The causes for the decay were mostly attributed to low quality of the sandstone and mortar.

Figure 1; The Macquarie Lighthouse is Australia's first lighthouse and its almost 200 year history served as the background for a computer-animated history lesson and associated experiments. Photo Copyright: Eric Fassbender.

Eventually, the deficiencies in construction were not tolerable anymore and from 1880 to 1883 a second lighthouse was built only 4 meters behind the old lighthouse (which was subsequently demolished). After the power supply of the lighthouse had been changed from coal-gas to kerosene in 1909, the lighthouse was connected to the main city electrical power supply in 1933. The lighthouse was automated in 1976 and de-manned in 1989. Despite being de-manned, it is still operational and is nowadays operated and maintained by the 'Australian Maritime Safety Authority' (AMSA, 2009). Public tours are organised by the 'Sydney Harbour Federation Trust' (SHFT, 2009).

Import of custom 3D model into 'The Elder Scrolls Construction Set'

To create a computer-animated lesson about the history of the Macquarie Lighthouse, I created a 3D model of the lighthouse in 3D Studio Max (3dsMax, 2009) from copies of the original blueprints. The blueprints (see Figure 2) were supplied by the Sydney Harbour Federation Trust and date back to the year 1883. After creating the 3D wireframe model of the Macquarie Lighthouse (see Figure 3 left) I added textures to the model (see Figure 3 right). As indicated earlier, I had evaluated a number of games and their respective modding capabilities and had settled on The Elder Scrolls Construction Set (TESCS).

To transfer the model into TESCS I had to save the model in the .nif format (NIF, 2009) that is used by TESCS for its 3D models. However, 3D Studio Max does not support direct export to this format and so I installed an export plug-in called Civilization IV MaxTools (Civ4Max, 2009). Originally this export plug-in was developed for the computer game Civilization IV but it also works for TESCS.

Once the .nif model of the Macquarie Lighthouse had been successfully exported from 3D Studio Max with the Civilization IV MaxTools export plug-in, I could insert the 3D lighthouse model into TESCS. New .nif files need to be stored in ..\Oblivion\Data\Meshes or a subfolder thereof and can then be accessed and used inside TESCS. Further technical details about the use and ex-/import of .nif files are supplied on the TESCS website (TESCS, 2009).

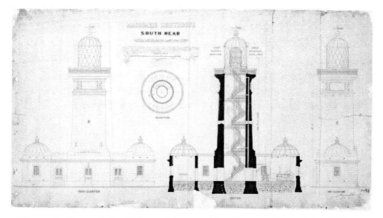

Figure 2; The original blueprints used for the creation of the 3D Model of the Macquarie Lighthouse. Blueprints supplied by the Sydney Harbour Federation Trust.

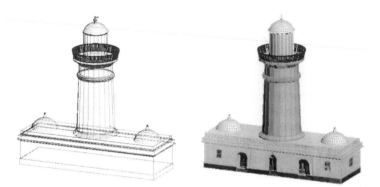

Figure 3; A 3D model of the Macquarie Lighthouse was created (left) and textures added in 3D Studio Max (right).

74

Figure 4; A simplified version of the survey map was used for the creation of a height model that served as a guide to create an accurate representation of the landscape surrounding the Macquarie Lighthouse. Source: Sydney Harbour Federation Trust.

Creation of Landscape

After the 3D model of the Macquarie Lighthouse had been created and inserted into TESCS, the surrounding landscape was reproduced as accurately as possible. This was achieved with the help of a survey map also supplied by the Sydney Harbour Federation Trust. However, the survey map was too cluttered with information and a simplified version (see Figure 4) was produced to serve as a guide for the creation of the landscape in TESCS.

The simplified survey map was used to create a height model of the area in 3D Studio Max. This height model was then also imported into TESCS (see pink landscape breaking through dark-green texture in Figure 5) and subsequently, the landscape surrounding the Macquarie Lighthouse was adjusted to fit the underlying height model. Figure 6 shows a close-up of the height model (pink), the landscape (dark-green 'grass' texture) and the Macquarie Lighthouse (right).

Figure 5; The Macquarie Lighthouse with an underlying height model (pink) of the real-world landscape.

Figure 6; Close-up of the height model (pink), the virtual landscape (dark-green 'grass' texture) and a corner of the Macquarie Lighthouse.

Figure 7 shows a red ellipsoid in the centre of the screenshot overlapping the pink height model and the dark-green textured model of the landscape inside TESCS. This red ellipsoid is the 'height' tool supplied by the landscape editor of TESCS. Upon clicking and moving the mouse upwards or downwards,

the selected section can be lifted or lowered respectively. Figure 8 shows
how a small part of the landscape was lifted (see red ellipsoid) to fit the
underlying height model. This lifting is shown exaggerated in this figure for
demonstration purposes.

Figure 7; The red ellipsoid in the centre of the screenshot shows the
'height tool' of TESCS.

Figure 8; Upon clicking and moving the computer mouse up and
down, the landscape can be raised or lowered.

In the distance of the above screenshots we can see a corner fence against the
texture of the sky. Four such corner fences were put up around the Macquarie
Lighthouse inside TESCS and the landscape within these boundaries (approx.
75 metres long & 45 metres wide) was lowered or raised with the landscape
editor (as described above) until it matched the imported height model
accurately.

Character and Dialog Development

After the 'stage' was prepared by modelling the Macquarie Lighthouse and the landscape, the next step was the creation of the virtual character that was going to present the history of the Macquarie Lighthouse to the users. For this purpose, TESCS supplies a range of powerful tools. TESCS includes a variety of pre-made characters that can be adapted to ones' personal requirements. Figure 9 shows one of the window dialogs that can be used to create and modify the virtual characters. The Avatar created for the delivery of the history of the Macquarie Lighthouse was named Mark Watson and is a fictitious descendant of the first lighthouse keeper Robert Watson. The Avatar was created as a middle-aged male human to give him the character of a believable lighthouse keeper of the time. Age, hair colour, symmetries of the face, eye colours and many more facial features were adjusted with the built-in tools (see the slider options in Figure 9 and others in further tabs) to create a friendly looking virtual lighthouse keeper.

Figure 9; Many facial features (e.g. Age, Hair Colour, etc.) were adjusted to create a friendly looking and welcoming virtual representation of a lighthouse keeper.

Figure 10; The Quest-System of TESCS can be used to create Avatar dialogs by grouping sentences (dashed box) into topics (solid box).

Once the Avatar was chosen and modified, the next step was to develop the dialog that the lighthouse keeper would use to deliver the history of the Macquarie Lighthouse to the users. For this purpose TESCS supplies a 'Quest System' in which dialogs and topics can be created. As can be seen in Figure 10, I organised the history of the lighthouse into eleven topics (see Editor ID in solid box in Figure 10) plus one introduction topic. These topics were used as meta-groups for the sentences listed under 'Response Details' (see dashed box in Figure 10). The information entered in these textboxes is then displayed as subtitles in the mod. However, in the case of the VirSchool (the virtual history lesson about the Macquarie Lighthouse), 'subtitles only' would not have been a very immersive experience and in order to increase the quality of the presentation (and level of immersion into the virtual environment) I decided to also supply auditory information by adding spoken language to the VirSchool history lesson.

The text with the historic information was spoken into an AKG C419 microphone, amplified by an Edirol UA-25 soundcard and recorded in Audacity (Audacity, 2011) on a Macbook Pro. Afterwards, the recorded audio files were converted to a 16 Bit (quantisation) mono .wav file at 44.1 KHz sample frequency to suit the specific file requirements that TESCS uses for the creation of the lip synchronisation of the Avatar. The reason for the usage of the .wav file format is that this format is a high-quality 'raw' format and thus offers the

very clear signals that TESCS needs for the creation of the lip synchronisation. However, because .wav files are comparatively big it would be impractical to use these files in a game (or the VirSchool history lesson in the present case). So, for later use in the mod, a mono .mp3 file at 64 kbit/s and at 44.1 KHz sample frequency is used which is much smaller in size (~ 1/10th of the size of the .wav file), yet, at this stage the loss of quality is not important anymore because the human ear is tricked by the psycho-acoustic compression method of the MP3 format and the signal does not need to have the same high quality that is necessary for the lip synchronisation process. For the present study, version 1.0.303 of TESCS was used and the lip synchronisation worked flawlessly. The later version 1.2.x introduced a bug that broke the utility that created the lip synch files for voiced dialogue; however, a bug fix is available as is the previous version 1.0.x (TESCS, 2011b).

Both audio files, the .wav and the .mp3, have to be placed in the folder that corresponds to the Avatar that was chosen (Imperial Male in our case). For the present project this folder was ..\Oblivion\Data\Sound\Voice\mqlight.esp\Imperial\M. These methods ensure that *what you read (subtitles) is what you hear (spoken text) and what you see (lip movements of the Avatar)*. The lip-synching method is an extremely powerful tool of TESCS and is described in detail on the website of TESCS (TESCS, 2011a).

Video

The next step in the creation of the experimental environment was to create videos of the topics as they were played and spoken in the VirSchool history lesson. One available software solution for screen recordings of 3D accelerated video game environments is Fraps (2009) - I used version 2.8.2 for the screen recordings. My reasons for choosing Fraps were that at the time of development of the VirSchool history lesson it was the fastest screen capture tool available for gaming environments. Furthermore, Fraps has the ability to record extreme wide-screen resolutions and especially this second capability was important for my experiment environment in which I used a resolution of 3072x768 pixels. This resolution is triple the amount of horizontal pixels that a standard desktop monitor displays (1024x768 pixels) and this triple resolution was required to display the video on a 3-monitor display system and a Reality Center (SGI 2009), (see Figures 13 and 14).

After recording the Avatar narration off the screen I created one master video in this wide screen format with Ulead Video Studio 10 and for the purpose of the experiment I embedded a number of background audio stimuli in the video thus creating several versions of the video, each 11 minutes and 38 seconds long. As mentioned earlier, the details of these experiments and the results are not the focus in this book chapter and I will therefore skip the explanations here. However, should the reader be interested in the details, please refer to Fassbender, Richards, Thompson, Bilgin & Taylor (2008) and Fassbender, Richards, Bilgin, Thompson & Heiden (2012) for more information about the experiments and their outcomes.

Figure 11 shows a screenshot of the finished computer-animated video narration of the history of the Macquarie Lighthouse in the 3072x768 pixel wide-screen resolution. The completed wide-screen resolution videos were then displayed on the 3-monitor display system and the Reality Center (see Figures 13 and 14), which are basically three screens positioned next to each other so that they create one wide-screen display. In order to supply the two display systems with the required wide-screen resolutions, I used a Matrox TripleHead2Go video signal splitter. Figure 12 shows the concept of this video splitter. The functionality of the TripleHead2Go is to simulate one big desktop display (e.g. the 3072x768 pixels as used for the present study) to the host operating system (Windows XP Professional, Service Pack 2). Subsequently, this resolution is split into three sections of equal size (1024x768 pixels) and output to three separate monitors (left, centre, right). Figure 13 and 14 show a scene from the original game (Oblivion) and the VirSchool history lesson displayed on the 3-monitor display system and the

Reality Center, respectively.

Figure 11; The finished computer-animated video narration of the history of the Macquarie Lighthouse in wide-screen resolution (3072x768 pixels).

Figure 12; A Matrox Triplehead2Go external video signal splitter extends the screen size to three monitors or other display devices. Source: http://www.matrox.com/graphics/en/products/gxm/th2go/

Figure 13; A scene from the original computer game 'The Elder Scrolls IV – Oblivion' running on three monitors. Photo: Eric Fassbender

Figure 14; The Reality Center - An immersive projection screen with a 150 Degree 'Field of view'. The Avatar (left) delivers the history of the Macquarie Lighthouse (rear-right) while one of the pilot-testers (front-right) watches and listens to the computer-animated history lesson wearing noise-cancelling headphones. Photo: Eric Fassbender

Summary

The VirSchool history lesson that served as a framework for associated experiments about the effect of music on memory in virtual environments was created with 'The Elder Scrolls Construction Set' (TESCS), a game-modding tool from the computer game 'The Elder Scrolls IV – Oblivion'.

The main reason why I chose TESCS over a number of other computer game construction sets was that it offers a first person perspective and the ability to easily create an avatar dialogue with lip synchronisation. TESCS fulfilled both of these criteria successfully and it was possible to achieve satisfying results within a very reasonable amount of time and the outcome of the development was of high quality. However, the capabilities of TESCS go far beyond the features that I have used for the creation of the VirSchool history lesson.

For example, TESCS offers the ability to create fully interactive virtual environments via a sophisticated quest system. Since entire landscapes can be created from scratch and custom 3D models imported into TESCS the options are practically limitless in terms of locations/sites that can be built and stories that can be developed. Thus, TESCS is a very capable tool for heritage applications not the least because of its ability to display extreme widescreen resolutions, which makes it a prime choice for multi-screen or multi-projector display systems.

On the down-side, the documentation of TESCS is a bit fragmented, thus the learning curve can be rather steep. Furthermore, TESCS has a few bugs and the interface itself is not very polished, which is understandable, as it was originally developed as an in-house development tool, rather than an end-user product. Ultimately, TESCS is a very powerful game modding tool that was used to develop a multi-million dollar game, thus, it should be possible to build any interactive, single-player virtual environment and it is recommended for anyone who wishes to build such environments.

The final verdict for me is that I would use TESCS again for a similar task. And this might not be too far away, as the next version of the Elder Scrolls series - Skyrim - has just been released at the time of writing this chapter. And with the game director Todd Howard stating that the Skyrim Creation Set "will be similar to the Oblivion Construction Set, but with better tools so that modders can make better mods" (SCS, 2011), it might in fact be very soon that I will embark on another modding journey.

References

Brown, A. (1992). Design experiments: Theoretical and methodological challenges in creating complex interventions in classroom settings. *The Journal of Learning Sciences, 2*(2), 141-178.

3dsMax (2009). *Autodesk 3D Studio Max.* Online. Retrieved January 27 2009 from http://www.autodesk.com/3dsmax

AMSA (2009). *Australian Maritime Safety Authority.* Online. Retrieved January 27 2009 from http://www.amsa.gov.au

Audacity (2011). *Audacity Sound Editor.* Online. Retrieved October 19 2011 from http://audacity.sourceforge.net

Bizzocchi, J., & Woodbury, R. F. (2003). *A case study in the design of interactive narrative: The subversion of the interface.* Simulation Gaming. 34(4), 550-568. doi:10.1177/1046878103258204

Casey, M., & Lowe, T. (2005). *Archaeological assessment of Macquarie Lightstation South Head*. Sydney: Sydney Harbour Federation Trust.

Civ4Max (2009). *Civilization IV MaxTools*. Online. Retrieved January 27 2009 from http://www.civfanatics.net/downloads/civ4/utility/CivilizationIV-MaxTools-v6.zip

Elder Scrolls (2011). *The Elder Scrolls Construction Set*. Online. Retrieved August 15 2011 from http://cs.elderscrolls.com

Fassbender, E., Richards, D., Bilgin, A., Thompson, W. F., & Heiden, W. (2012). *Virschool: The effect of background music and immersive display systems on memory for facts learned in an educational virtual environment*. Computers & Education. 58(1). 490-500. doi:10.1016/j.compedu.2011.09.002

Fassbender, E., Richards, D., Thompson, W. F., Bilgin, A., & Taylor, A. (2008). *The effect of music on learning in virtual environments - initial results*. In International conference on auditory display. Paris, France.

Fraps (2009). *Fraps - Real-time video capture & benchmarking*. Online. Retrieved January 29 2009 from http.//www.fraps.com

MacGregor, J., & Leung, S. (2009). *Pathfinding strategy for multiple non-playing characters in 2.5 D game worlds*. LNCS. 5670. 351-362.

Neverwinter Nights (2009). *Aurora Neverwinter Toolset*. Online. Retrieved January 27 2009 from http://nwn.bioware.com/builders

NIF (2009). *NifTools*. Online. Retrieved January 27 2009 from http://niftools.sourceforge.net/wiki/Nif_Format

Reid (1988). *From dusk till dawn*. South Melbourne: Macmillan

SCS (2011). *Skyrim Creation Set*. Online. Retrieved 11 November 2011 from http://elderscrolls.wikia.com/wiki/Construction_Set_(Skyrim)

Second Life (2011). *Second Life*. Online. Retrieved 19 October 2011 from http://www.secondlife.com

SGI (2009). *SGI® reality center™ at QMI reality works enhances large-scale manufacturing and public works projects*. SGI.SHFT (2009). Sydney Harbour Federation Trust . Online. Retrieved January 27 2009 from http://www.harbourtrust.gov.au

TESCS (2009). *The Elder Scrolls Construction Set*. Online. Retrieved January 27 2009 from http://cs.elderscrolls.com/constwiki/index.php/NIF_Files; and http://cs.elderscrolls.com/constwiki/index.php/Working_With_Nifs_101_:_An_Introduction

TESCS (2011a). *The Elder Scrolls Construction Set - Audio Settings For Dialogue Video Tutorial* .Online. Retrieved October 19 2011 from http://cs.elderscrolls.com/constwiki/index.php/Audio_Settings_For_Dialogue_Video_Tutorial

TESCS (2011b). *The Elder Scrolls Construction Set - Avatar Lip-Syncing*. Online. Retrieved March 27 2011 from http://cs.elderscrolls.com/constwiki/index.php/TES_Construction_Set

Torque (2009). *Torque Game Engine*. Online. Retrieved January 27 2009 from http://www.garagegames.com

Chapter 4

Game Mods,

Engines,

and

Architecture

87

Kevin R. Conway

88

Game Mods, Engines and Architecture

Kevin R. Conway kscc38@hotmail.com

Introduction

"The building-industry is one of the few industries that lack the possibility of using full-scale prototypes to evaluate and test their designs." (Achten, Roelen, Boekholt, Turksma, & Jessurun, 1999).

An exciting new architectural visualization technique is being experimented with that promises affordable and relatively easy real-time walk through visualizations. The technique is based on the ubiquitous video game and its built-in game engine and editor. With game engine and editor, it is possible to insert digital models and in a few minutes be walking around in a virtual world experiencing an architectural design in a way that is not possible with traditional architectural representations.

Video games, such as *Unreal Tournament, Crysis* and *Half-Life* are readily available, inexpensive and include the game engine and editor in the purchase price. When used with familiar modeling and image software such as *3D Max, SketchUp* and *Photoshop*, real-time explorable architectural visualizations ranging from massing studies to fully rendered environments are possible.

Although physical architectural models have traditionally been used to evaluate architectural design, a physical model's scale, detail, materialization and point of view can limit a model's usefulness. A game engine based architectural visualization, on the other hand, allows a viewer to experience an architectural design at full scale and from a realistic point of view. Accurate materials and lighting can be rendered providing an opportunity for a much more comprehensive evaluation of a design. These features suggest that game engine based architectural visualization could a useful tool for the design process.

Video Games

It is hard to understand the potential of game engines and editors to create architectural visualizations without understanding video games. There are many types and genres of video games from arcade style side-scrollers to fantasy role playing games but the genre that offers the most opportunities for architectural visualization is the First Person Shooter (FPS).

The FPS genre is very popular and has been very successful. For example, the video game *Call of Duty: Modern Warfare* which was released Nov. 10, 2009, sold approximately 4.7 million copies in three days, making it the biggest launch in history across all forms of entertainment including movies, music and everything else. (Orry, 2009)

The FPS genre focuses on gun and projectile weapon based combat from a first-person perspective. Players experience the action as if through their own eyes. Players move through virtual FPS worlds following any path they choose, looking in any direction they choose and possibly being attacked from any direction. It is this freedom of action that provides the potential for real-time architectural visualizations.

Originally, each video game was written as a self-contained software program but during the evolution of video games an important development occurred: video games became modular. To reduce the effort required to create additional video games, game developers began writing software with rendering, physics, sound and etc. as a separate module from the artwork and gameplay logic. Game developers could then create entirely new games just be creating new artwork (models, animations and textures) and defining new gameplay logic. The software module that performs rendering, physics and similar functions has come to be known as the "Game Engine".

The FPS game engine incorporates all the features necessary to make effective architectural visualizations. These features include: first person point-of-view, gravity (that is, a default connection to the ground plane), collision detection (to prevent walking through walls and so forth), and an emphasis on realism. These features are built into the game engine and managed by the game editor, which makes the game engine a natural platform from which to create architectural visualizations.

The game editor is a software tool that allows the game designer to import digital models, textures, animations and other game assets into the game engine. The editor also allows the game designer to setup and manipulate lighting and physics effects. Finally, the game editor allows the game designer to adjust and fine tune various settings that control the "look" and "feel" of the game's virtual world.

Game Engines and Editors

It is easy confuse the game engine with the actual game. The relationship between the game engine and the game is analogous to the relationship between the automobile engine/chassis and the automobile body and interior. Like the automobile body and interior, the "game" is the part that the user interacts with and is the part that differentiates one game from any other games. Just as automobile engines/chassis are regularly used with different bodies to create different car models, so are game engines used to create different games. For example, the *Unreal Engine (Unreal Tournament)* has been used to create dozens of different games by many different developers. (List of Unreal Engine Games, 2011)

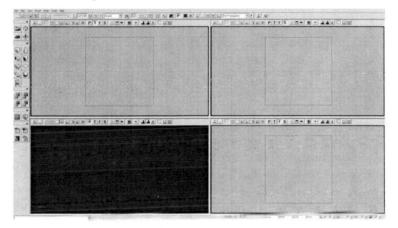

Figure 1; Unreal Game Engine Editor (author).

A game engine provides rendering, lighting, sound, physics and artificial intelligence (AI). Rendering includes the processes that take digital models and 3D geometry and transform these into virtual representations in the game world. Through various mathematical transformations, 3D geometry appears solid, acquires texture and color, receives light and simulates first person perspective. In a FPS game the renderer must do the rendering in real time with a constantly changing viewpoint and input to create an illusion that the player is occupying another world that is being interacted with.

The amount of these calculations is staggering and would be impossible without multi-core processors, huge data storage and graphics cards in addition to the sophisticated coding behind each game and game engine. Fortunately, many modern personal computers provide these features and will run most video games without problem.

One important goal of game engines is to maximize the display frame rate. Frame rates in video games refer to the frequency at which the image is re-displayed. Frame rates are typically measured in Frames Per Second (FPS). Slow frame rates appear "jerky" and can negatively impact game play. Game designers generally seek to achieve a minimum of 30 FPS, which is the frame rate most movies are presented at.

Game Lighting

Believable lighting is crucial to effective architectural visualizations whether visualizing massing studies or through fully rendered final presentations. Video games provide two basic types of lighting: static lighting and dynamic lighting. Static lighting is lighting that does not change during gameplay. These may include sunlight and other light sources that will not be turned off and on or otherwise changed during the course of playing the game. Dynamic lighting is lighting that does change during gameplay. These may include lights that can be turned on and off, lights that move and lights that change color.

Because static lighting does not change, static lighting effects can be pre-calculated when the game is being created rather than be calculated during gameplay thereby saving computer resources. Pre-calculating static lighting is called light mapping. Game engines use light maps to increase game processing efficiency. Creating light maps is sometimes called "baking", which is the game designer's slang for processing static lighting to produce light maps. To produce light maps, lighting for only static lights is calculated and the resulting brightness, shadows and other characteristics are used to create special textures called light maps that are then overlaid on the existing textures in the game world. The light maps are blended with existing textures to create the lighting effect while the game is being created. In this way, all the shadows, hotspots, color shifts and so forth, from static lights are already calculated and incorporated into the game before gameplay

Some game engines are even beginning to incorporate advanced global illumination calculations in the light mapping. Global illumination algorithms calculate not only direct illumination, but also indirect lighting reflected and refracted by other surfaces in the scene. Images rendered using global illumination algorithms appear much more photorealistic than images rendered using only direct illumination algorithms. However, global illumination is much more computationally expensive and, therefore, very time consuming to generate. By pre-calculating global illumination and baking the results into a light map, there is almost no impact on the computational overhead during gameplay. Game engines that incorporate global illumination dramatically improve the potential for photorealistic environments.

MIPS and LOD

Textures are very important for making 3D scenes look real. Textures are image files representing surface materials that are applied to objects in a scene. There can be many textures in a scene and textures can take up a lot of computer memory. Not all textures can be stored in memory at one time, so textures are loaded and unloaded multiple times during gameplay. Managing texture sizes, use and loading is very important for optimizing and maintaining an acceptable frame rate during gameplay.

Detailed information about textures and other 3D graphics topics is beyond the scope of this article but an excellent source of additional information is Real Time Rendering, Third Edition by Tomas Akenine-Moller, Eric Haines, and Naty Hoffman and published by AK Peters (2008)

One technique used to reduce texture memory size is to use MIP maps. MIP is an acronym for the Latin phrase "Multum In Parvo", which means "much in a small space". MIP maps are a pre-calculated and optimized collection of incremental resolution texture images for each texture in a scene. MIP maps are used to increase rendering speed while minimizing aliasing artifacts. Aliasing artifacts are small visual distortions in the screen image resulting image calculations, frequently from rounding errors in the algorithms used. Typically each incremental MIP map image is at one half the resolution of the previous MIP map image. MIP map collections typically contain eight incremental resolution texture images. MIP maps can be generated automatically or manually, however, most game engines that support MIP maps can generate the required set of images automatically. .

In most game engines, as the distance between textures and the camera increase, the game engine will substitute lower resolution MIP maps to maintain acceptable framerates. For a variety of reasons, reducing a texture resolution in real time may lead to texture distortion and aliasing artifacts. With MIP mapping, the texture is rescaled at various resolutions in advance. Pre-calculating MIP maps results in more accurate rescaling that reduces texture distortion. During gameplay, the game engine determines the texture's distance from the camera and then displays the best resolution texture for the distance. Because distant textures require less detail, lower resolution textures with smaller file sizes can be loaded resulting in improved performance.

Similar to MIP mapping are Level of Detail (LOD) systems that use algorithms to scale the geometric complexity of 3D models based on the distance from the model geometry to the camera. LOD systems provide the ability to dynamically alter the number of polygons used to draw a model on screen at any given moment. For example, when a model is seen far off in the distance, and displays a height of 10 pixels on screen, the model's full 3000 polygons (for example) are not necessary to render the model, a much reduced number of polygons (like 300 for example) would be sufficient for display. The difference between 300 polygons and 3000 polygons when displayed at 10 pixels high will not be discerned by a viewer and will dramatically save computer resources and improve frame rates.

LOD systems use a couple of strategies to reduce polygon counts; one strategy is to pre-calculate and save multiple versions of a model at incrementally reduced complexity; reduced complexity LOD models on screen depending on the distance the model is from the viewer or how many polygons are being displayed at once. However, more newer and sophisticated systems will dynamically reduce the number of polygons on screen at any each moment, for any given model in real time.

When first introduced, single layer texture maps made a huge improvement in game visuals, however; despite these improvements, game visuals, were still rather flat and bland. Nowadays, modern game engines rely on multiple texture layers to create the sophisticated visual effects demanded by gamers. Visual effects such as light maps, decals, normal maps and bump maps all require multiple layered textures to be effective. Rendering multiple texture layers originally required an individual computation pass for each texture, however; this degraded frame rates significantly and game play suffered. With the advent of multiple core graphics cards, multiple texture layers can generally be rendered in a single pass by rendering each texture layer as a semi-transparent layer on top of each previous texture. This technique allows many special effects including textures that can appear to move, pulse and/or have shadows.

Textures are loaded and stored in special memory caches designated for that purpose. Because of the file size and importance of textures, texture cache management is vital to efficient game engines. Like other types of memory caches, active use of cached textures is good, but it is very inefficient to have textures being constantly swapped in and out of the texture cache. Inefficient caching can result in the entire texture cache being dumped which will require all of the textures to be reloaded at the next texture request. Inefficient texture drawing and reloading can significantly reduce frame rates and produce what is known as image "stutter".

Fog

Many video games include fog as a visual effect. Although fog may seem like a minor special effect, it is actually very useful for successful visualizations. Game engines are set up to only render objects when they are within a certain distance of the camera. This distance, called the "clipping plane" may seem distant in the game but the sudden rendering of an object when the object crosses the clipping plane makes the object appear to "pop" into view and this can be annoying or even jarring. Fog is used to fade out the world in the distance, so models and scene geometry do not abruptly pop into view when they cross the farthest clipping plane. The models and geometry may still be abruptly rendered when they cross the clipping plane but the fog masks the popping so that it is much less jarring. Fog is achieved by blending the polygon's colors with grey, based on polygon's distance from the camera.

Anti-Aliasing

Smooth edges in an image are critical to creating realistic appearing 3D images on the screen, but screen images are made up grids of pixels so that diagonal and curved edges may look jagged. Anti-aliasing creates the illusion that a jagged edge is smooth. Anti-aliasing does not actually smooth any of the edges in images anti-aliasing actually blends edge pixels and the adjacent pixels in a way that fools the eye into seeing a smooth edge.

Figure 2; Examples of aliasing (upper line) and anti-aliasing (lower line) (author)

Jagged edges are caused by limitations in a computer screen, regardless of what display technology is used because all current display technologies are based on pixels arranged in a grid or matrix. Monitors can produce smooth straight horizontal or vertical lines; however, curved lines and diagonal lines at any angle cannot be produced without some jaggedness. Because of the pixel grid arrangement, diagonal lines are drawn as a stair-stepped arrangement of pixels that approximate a diagonal line. Circles, arcs and other shapes are drawn in a similar way also with resulting jaggedness.

Anti-aliasing is line smoothing strategy based on various algorithms that attempt to interpolate shades of color between the jagged edges of a line or shape to create the illusion of a smoother edge. Although generally effective, the additional computation required by anti-aliasing processes can reduce frame rates and occasionally result in small unintended image artifacts.

The most common application of anti-aliasing in current video games and game engines is Full Scene Anti-Aliasing (FSAA). FSAA refers to the application of anti-aliasing to the entire screen and not just to certain parts of an image. FSAA performs anti-aliasing calculations for every frame, from the top to the bottom of the screen to remove jagged edges for the entire screen.

The level of FSAA is referred to by the number of samples taken to determine the color of an interpolated pixel. FSAA may be referred to as 2x, 4x, 6x or 8x. Higher sample rates result in better image quality but slower frame rates. FSAA 2x and FSAA 4x have been the most common but FSAA 6x and FSAA 8x are becoming more common as graphics cards become increasingly powerful.

Physics

In the virtual game world, objects and characters must accurately respond to gravity, collisions, acceleration, and inertia. Game physics are managed by the physics engine, which is a component of the game engine. The physics engine provides general physics rules to simulate real-world physics by default; but these default physics rules can be adjusted or overridden for certain effects. The ability to override standard physics rules can provide designers with intriguing possibilities.

Most game engines include a particle effects generator that creates many of the special effects like fire, smoke and explosions. Particles are very small renderable objects. To produce these effects, a group of particles must be created and their behavior and characteristics defined. As each particle moves during game play the interactions between the particles and the rest of the game world are calculated for each frame in real time. Physics affect each particle and are included in the calculations, these calculations can be computationally very demanding.

Sound and Music

Sound and music in games have become increasingly important in recent years due to both the benefits they provide and improvements in the technology used to create and control the sound and music. Four, five and six speaker surround systems are now affordable and common.

Sound spatialization is very important to game play and describes characteristics of in-game sound generation that allow players to identify the distance, orientation and source of an in-game sound. Spatialization is achieved by using multiple sound channels and by using the 3D distance from the sound source to the camera to determine the volume for each channel. Spatialization also includes obstruction and occlusion of sound which are very important to creating realistic simulations of sound. Obstruction occurs when something between the observer and the sound source completely blocks any sound from being heard, so that any sound that is heard will be indirect sound that has been reflected off walls or other objects. Occlusion occurs when something between the observer and the sound source partially blocks any sound from being heard so that any sound heard will be muted and/or distorted from passing through the object depending on the obstruction's composition and the observer's distance to both the obstruction and the sound source. (Murphy & Neff, 2011)

Sound editors are like game editors and allow game designers to construct and then create the sound maps necessary for spatialization. A sound map uses a simplified representation of the game geometry to locate the various sources of sound within the game world. Simplified geometry is used to create the sound maps rather than the original geometry because the more complex original geometry is not necessarily more effective when simulating sound environments. Surfaces and objects in the sound map are tagged with attributes that describe how the surfaces and objects modify in-game sounds. Because objects and surfaces are individually tagged with sound attributes, when objects move during gameplay sound can change dynamically in response.

Music is used during game play to establish mood and narrative structure. Many video games have complex, original soundtracks similar to those in movies. There have even been concerts that focus on video game music including one in Seattle celebrating the music of the video game Halo 3 ODST (Liu, 2009).

Music can be incorporated into video games by two primary methods. The first method is to include standard music files (WAV, MP3 or OGG for example). These provide pre-recorded music and are easy to incorporate (but must be licensed or royalty free). However, using prerecorded music files can be computationally expensive because the data transfer of music from memory may compete with graphics processing and possibly impact on frame rates.

The second method is to create a Musical Instrument Digital Interface (MIDI) track. A MIDI track contains instructions allowing the computer to generate music. Although, MIDI generally uses less memory, MIDI may not use hardware and software resources effectively.

Some game engines also offer dynamic music capability which is the ability to change the tempo of the music to coordinate with the pace of the game. For example, a game engine could establish a slow tempo during exploration and transition sequences but use a faster tempo during action sequences. Using pre-recorded music tracks it is difficult to change and coordinate the music's tempo dynamically during gameplay; however, using a MIDI track makes it much easier to change the music's tempo dynamically. (Collins, 2008),

Multiplayer/Network Support

One of the big reasons for the popularity of video games, especially the FPS genre, is the opportunity to play online against other players. When connected to the internet and in multiplayer mode, players can log on to a specific game and play against others in a shared virtual world. Using multiplayer/network support technology, multiple persons can share and interact in a virtual world while aware of each other's presence in the virtual world. In FPS games this sharing and interacting is from a first person point of view and in real time.

Because video games are meant to have a broad popular appeal for a wide age range, multiplayer/network support was been designed to be easy to setup and maintain. Whether hosting a game or just logging in to play, the setup procedures usually only require a couple minutes to accomplish and because it usually id setup using the internet it is available to almost everyone. In addition, users can also choose to establish an ad hoc Local Area Network (LAN). The LAN setup is the basis of wildly popular "LAN parties" where several to hundreds of users gather in one location with their computers to play the same video game against each other. Multiplayer/network support in video games is so easy that it suggests possibilities for architectural visualization to increase team collaboration even when team members may be in different cities or even different countries.

Collaboration among the parties involved in a project is crucial to the success of a project. However, the cost to attend meetings, the locations of team members, time constraints and other factors can prevent team members from getting together as often as might be preferred. Game engine based visualizations can address this issue because of networked multiplayer support. For example, an architect could host a "game" running an architectural visualization and team members located anywhere in the world could log on to the game and participate in the architectural visualization. There are also methods to communicate with the participants while they are in the game. However, this does require that each participant have a copy of the video game installed on their local computer.

Another option available with some game engines and editors is to compile the completed visualization to run on a web page. This option does not require that the video game software be installed on local computers. These options could greatly enhance team collaboration on projects from the earliest concept stage through construction.

Modding

It is not hard to imagine that after being confronted with incredible worlds inside video games that some gamers wanted to create and experience worlds that they imagined. At first this was very difficult but some gamers persisted and made some progress. A video game released in 1981 called *Castle Wolfenstein* about Nazis and their hidden fortress was modified to become *Castle Smurfenstein with Smurfs* replacing the Nazis.

Figure 4; Source: The first 'Official' *Castle Wolffenstein* Home Page,
http://www.evl.uic.edu/aej/smurf.html, retrieved 10/16/2011

The process of modifying video games has come to be known as "modding".
Modding was very difficult when video games first became popular because
no effort had been made by the game developers to support modding.
Game developers had not anticipated any interest in modifying their games.
Modding developed after *Castle Smurfenstein* because the video game
developers began creating modular games based on game engines. As video
games became more popular, some game developers stopped creating their
own game engines and started licensing successful game engines from other
game developers.

The first game engines released did not have associated game editors. Before
game editors were developed the process of modding a game was time
consuming and tedious. Modding required good programing skills because the
actual game code had to be accessed to make the mods. The game developers
had some in-house software tools to create games but these tools were not easy
to use and the game developers did not release these tools. Out of necessity some
modders created basic editing tools to access the game code and released these
editing tools to the public. However, the early game editing tools (both the
commercial and the amateur) were inefficient, buggy and incomplete. Modding
a game frequently required processing new game assets through multiple
software packages to prepare and insert the assets into the game engine.

The original game editors were released almost as an after-thought, but as
interest in modding increased, serious development was directed at the game

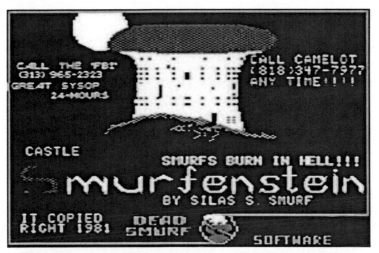

Figure 5; Source: The first 'Official' *Castle Smurfenstein* Home
Page, http://www.evl.uic.edu/aej/smurf.html, retrieved 10/16/2011.

editor. Currently many video games come with integrated and sophisticated
"what you see is what you get" (WYSIWYG) game editors.

Current game editors can manipulate textures, models, animations, scripts,
music and other required game assets. In-editor play testing is now possible
which greatly speeds up game development. Some editors include integrated
tools for creating complex textures, animations, scripts and cut scenes. Game
editors now recognize many standard file formats rather than requiring
conversion of models and artwork into their own proprietary formats. Many
editors can now seamlessly import models and textures (and sometimes
models with textures already attached). Finally, editors are usually thoroughly
tested and de-bugged and function with minimal problems.

Level Design

FPS games are divided into gameplay areas called "levels". When a game is
being played, the computer only processes data contained within the level the
player is currently active in. A player usually moves progressively through the
levels with each new level representing a new goal or challenge. Although a level
may represent a specific area, theme or goal, a level is also a means to manage
computer resources to achieve the best performance. Architectural visualizations
would usually be accomplished in one level although large interior spaces might
have to be organized as different levels. Urban design visualizations, on the
other hand, could also be developed using game engines and might require

multiple levels depending on the size of the area being modeled.

When a game is modded, the user either modifies an existing level or creates a new level. A level usually starts with creating the terrain. Terrain can have mountains, deserts, valleys, roads, lakes, rivers, cliffs and so forth. Terrain will also have trees, plants, grass and other vegetation. Each terrain will usually have a skybox associated with it. A skybox is an enclosing volume with a sky image texture applied to the inside surface (the game side surface). The terrain and skybox together creates the basic game world.

With the basic level established, objects are added to represent buildings, vehicles, rocks and other structures. Each object added to the level is a 3D mesh. Meshes are created in modeling software like *3D Max* and imported into the game engine using the game editor for placement into the level. Complicated objects may be made from several meshes. Meshes that are repeated in a level are generally instanced. Instancing means that the description of the mesh object is loaded into memory once and every repeated instance of the mesh requires only the location, rotation and scale of the object in addition to a reference to the originally loaded description of the mesh object. This can save a tremendous amount of memory when used effectively. Every object, automobile or building in a level is one or more meshes.

102

Using Textures

After the game objects are created, textures for the objects must be created. Some textures may be provided with some of the game editors but they tend to be overly dramatic (as befits an action game) and not suitable for an architectural visualization. Therefore, it will probably be necessary to create custom textures. Creating textures is performed outside of the game editor in graphics software (like *Photoshop*) and imported into the game engine. Creating custom high quality textures can be the most time consuming part of creating a mod.

There are two basic types of textures that can be created: tileable textures and UV textures. Tileable textures are meant to be repeated on a surface (tiled). Some types of materials are well suited for tileable textures such as brick, ceramic tiles, hardwood floors and etc. There are special software packages that are designed to create tileable textures and *Photoshop* has several tools that are helpful for creating tileable textures.

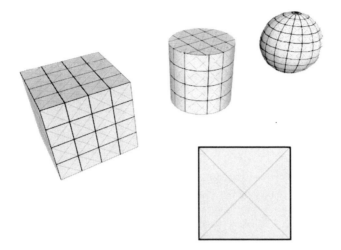

Figure 6; Examples of tileable texture and tiles objects (author).

After the game objects are created, textures for the objects must be created. Some textures may be provided with some of the game editors but they tend to be overly dramatic (as befits an action game) and not suitable for an architectural visualization. Therefore, it will probably be necessary to create custom textures. Creating textures is performed outside of the game editor in graphics software (like *Photoshop*) and imported into the game engine. Creating custom high quality textures can be the most time consuming part of creating a mod.

Tileable textures are relatively easy to create and map (apply) to an object but are subject to potential distortion based on the shape of the object the texture is being mapped to. Most 3D modeling software and game editors support several methods of mapping based on primitive shapes like cube, cylinder, and sphere. These additional mapping methods reduce the potential distortion when mapping. Organic shapes may require UV textures and mapping.

UV textures are created for specific surfaces or objects and may not involve much repetition. UV textures can be applied to three-dimensional objects by "unwrapping" the object's surface. When a surface is unwrapped it is laid flat as a two-dimensional shape. While XYZ coordinates apply to three-dimensional objects, a different coordinate system is required for an unwrapped surface that will be reapplied to a three-dimensional object. UV coordinates are used for unwrapped surfaces. UV coordinates allow a surface to be reapplied to an object accurately.

Figure 7; Example of a 3D object unwrapped (KRC).

After an object has been unwrapped, the resulting two-dimensional shape can not only be painted to represent any required material but can also be painted to represent wear and tear like dirt, stains, and surface changes. Complex combinations of material that are not possible with tiled textures can be painted on the shapes. Completed UV textures are then imported into the game engine using the game editor and reapplied to the original object. What can be done with UV textures is basically unlimited.

There is one other specialized type of texture that is used with some 3D models. Detailed, high-resolution meshes can have a large impact on memory usage. One technique to reduce the memory requirements of high-resolution 3D models employed by game designers and modders is to use "normal maps". Normal mapping begins with a complex object modeled at very high resolution on which textures have been applied mapped. The textured object is then lit and the lighting patterns of shadow and highlight are saved as a lightmap texture that is overlaid over the original object texture. These two textures are then combined and saved to create a normal map texture. A low resolution model of the original high-resolution object is then created. When combined with the normal map texture, the low resolution model looks as detailed as the high resolution model but with a greatly reduced memory size. There is software available to help create normal maps.

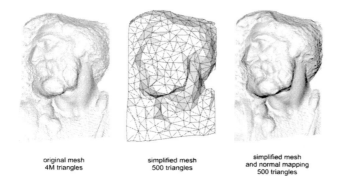

original mesh
4M triangles

simplified mesh
500 triangles

simplified mesh
and normal mapping
500 triangles

Figure 8; Example of a normal map (Normal Mapping, Wikipedia, http://en.wikipedia.org/wiki/Normal_ mapping, retrieved Oct. 11, 2011).

Setting Up Lighting

With meshes and textures created, imported and placed in the level, the modder next sets up lighting. Lighting in games is a combination of static lighting and dynamic lighting. Static lights do not change and dynamic lights can move or change. Some game engines also support creating meshes and/or textures that are light emitting.

Lights may be point lights, spot lights or directional lights (like the sun). Light emitting meshes and textures can be used to simulate a variety of fixture types like fluorescent fixtures, globes or neon lighting. Lighting is often the second most time consuming part of creating a level after texture creation

It can be useful to begin by placing the primary light source which may be a directional light representing the sun. Static lights representing architectural lighting can be placed after the primary light source. Next, various accent lights and fill lights may be placed. Finally, any dynamic lights that are required may be placed. Lighting the level is usually an iterative process that requires examination form many points of view and then adjustment until complete.

Adding Sound

Sound effects can be very useful in creating a degree of immersiveness in an architectural visualization. Having street noises outside a building or crowd noises inside a building help the viewer transition from looking at an object to experiencing the object.

Sound effects are relatively easy to add to a level and can include everything from ambient nature sounds to creaking doors. Sound files are loaded into a level and generally attached to an object or to a location. Several variables can be adjusted including range and fall-off method. Many sound effects will be in stereo and will contribute to specialization.

Music can also be readily included in a level. However, the designer should consider that music can be emotionally powerful and therefore manipulative. Also, music preference is highly personal so that music choices made by the designer may not resonate with the audience. Finally, if the music selected is not royalty free then it must be licensed for use.

Animation

If an animation is required, the animation can be created in most 3D modeling software (like *3D Max*) and imported into the game engine using the game editor. Animations can be continuous or can be triggered in a variety of ways including by proximity or key press. For simple actions like opening doors, animations may not be required because some game editors have built-in routines to handle simple movements and rotations. However, complex actions may require animations. Calatrava's Milwaukee Art Museum with its movable brise soleil would be a good candidate for an animation.

Player Start

Games generally require that a "Player Start" or player's point-of-view camera be located in the level. The "Player Start" or player's point-of-view camera represents the initial location of the player at the start of a game. The location of the Player Start is very important to establishing the narrative and context of the architectural visualization. When locating the Player Start, a location and view direction should be chosen that supports the exploration that is to follow.

Should the Player Start be some distance away so that the proposed building slowly comes into view? The Player Start can be up close and framing the proposed building perhaps simulating a rendering. The Player Start could be inside the proposed building or outside. The Player Starts represents the audience's first impression so the designer should choose it carefully.

Architectural Visualization

The image below is a drawing of a proposed house for Constance Gillis and her husband designed by Bruce Goff in 1945. This design was chosen for an architectural visualization because of the unique design and because there are only six original conceptual drawings of the design (3 plans, 2 elevation options and a section). Creating an architectural visualization of this design allows one to walk around the design and consider it from points of view not represented by the extant drawings. Likewise, it is also possible to enter the design and explore the interior.

The 3D model for this visualization was created in SketchUp. Textures were found and created and applied to the model in *SketchUp*. The completed model with textures was then exported from *SketchUp* using the FBX file format. The FBX file was then imported into the *Unity3D* game engine using the *Unity 3D* editor. Finally, the individual texture files were imported into Unity 3D. The texture placement coordinates used in *SketchUp* were included in the FBX file so that the textures are correctly placed on the model in *Unity 3D*.

This architectural visualization was intended as a demonstration of quick visualization techniques that might be used during design development so the landscaping and terrain was kept very simple. Finally, when the visualization was complete, it was compiled as a stand-alone executable file so that it could be distributed on a disk, emailed, or downloaded from a website.

Figure 9; Bruce Goff's proposed design for the Constance Gillis House 1945 (The Art Institute of Chicago, Ryerson & Burnham Archives: Archival Image Collection).

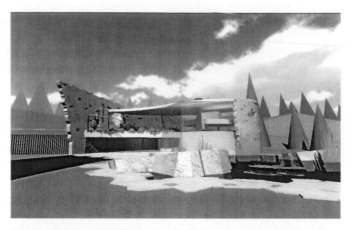

Figure 10; View of front. Bruce Goff's proposed design for the Constance Gillis house visualized in the *Unity 3D* game engine (author).

Figure 11; Detail. Bruce Goff's proposed design for the Constance Gillis house visualized in the *Unity 3D* game engine (author)

Figure 12; View of back. Bruce Goff's proposed design for the Constance Gillis house visualized in the *Unity 3D* game engine (author).

Figure 13; View from interior. Bruce Goff's proposed design for the Constance Gillis house visualized in the *Unity 3D* game engine (author).

Conclusion

As game engine based architectural visualization becomes more familiar to architects and designers, there are several additional features that could be added to the game engines to make them more useful. An accurate method to represent sunlight based on the proposed design's actual geographic location would be helpful. This would include positioning based on latitude, longitude and compass direction. Included with this should be the ability to model the sunlight based on specific days and times and to cycle through the sun's position for the entire year so that daylighting and shadows can be evaluated. Another potential addition would be the ability to model terrain from specific site data and contours. Currently, sites can only be modeled by eye. Software or other techniques that could convert contours or point data into the height maps that game editors use would significantly increase the usefulness of game engines for architectural visualizations.

Finally, although multiplayer network support allows multiple users to experience a game engine based architectural visualization at the simultaneously, there is currently no means to "mark-up" or notate the visualization for later reference. One approach might be to modify a game weapon to act like spray paint. Users could "spray" their comments on the building in-game to be recorded for later reference.

Game engine based architectural visualization provides a powerful tool because it allows architects and designers to more fully evaluate, understand and communicate architectural design.

Because full scale models of proposed designs are not practical, real-time walk-throughs can provide many of the benefits of a full scale model would and a few additional benefits. These additional benefits include the enhanced collaboration possible with multiplayer network support, the ability to modify designs quickly and the ability to easily generate multiple design variations relatively easily.

However, the biggest potential advantage is the cost. A full size model of a building could be as expensive as the actual building would be (if it was even practical to build a full size model of a building). On the other hand, a game engine based real-time walkthrough requires an initial investment of fifty dollars for the game and a few hours to import a 3D model and setup the visualization.

References

Achten, H., Roelen, W., Boekholt, J.-T., Turksma, A., & Jessurun, J. (1999). Virtual Reality in the Design Studio: The Eindhoven Perspective, Architectural Computing from Turing to 2000. *eCAADe Conference Proceedings*, (pp. pp. 169-177). Liverpool (UK).

Collins, K. (2008). *Game sound: an introduction to the history, theory, and practice of video.* Cambridge, Massachusetts, USA: MIT Press

Liu, M. (2009, 01 23). *Seattle Times - Music / Nightlife.* Retrieved 8 September, 2011, from Seattle Times: http://seattletimes.nwsource.com/html/musicnightlife/2008660692_zmus23videogameslive.html

Murphy, D., & Neff, F. (2011). Spatial Sound for Computer Games and Virtual Reality. In M. Grimshaw, *Game Sound Technology and Player Interaction: Concepts and Developments* (pp. 287-312). Hershey, PA: Information Science Reference.

Orry, J. (2009, 11 12). *Modern Warfare 2 sells 4.7 million day one in U.S. and UK.* Retrieved 2 September, 2011, from http://www.videogamer.com: http://www.videogamer.com/xbox360/cod_modern_warfare_2/news/modern_warfare_2_sells_4_7_million_day_one_in_us_and_uk.html

Wikipedia.(2011). *List of Unreal Engine Games.* (2011, 8 30). Retrieved 2 September, 2011, from Wikipedia, the Free Encyclopedia. http://en.wikipedia.org/wiki/List_of_Unreal_Engine_games

Chapter 5

Teaching

Mods

with

Class

113

Erik Champion

114

Teaching Mods with Class

Erik Champion, Digital Humanities Lab Denmark,
IT-Parken, Wienerbygningen, Helsingforsgade 14,
8200 Aarhus N, Aarhus University, echa@adm.au.dk

Exactly What It Says, Not What You Think

This title refers to teaching games through mods, in classes for university students. I did not, unfortunately, teach how to design classy game mods; rather, with the students we used game modding to understand game design. Game mods are quicker to build so they can be more easily incorporated into short game design courses. They can also be used to encourage students to think beyond conventional games, conceptually and in terms of equipment. While some of the following projects are not resolved, they may inspire you to push some of the design thinking further.

In the game design classes that I taught in two universities, from 2005, to 2008, I marked the students on their level design proposal, their presentation of the final level design, and the level design itself. However, this final component had two subcomponents; my assessment of the level design, and their assessment of another student group's level design. This last subcomponent mark involved marking them for completing the test and analysis of another group's level, and my mark of their own level design. At the time I was happy to get that far within a traditional university system, now I would rather incorporate even more group and personal assessment.

For their assessment of the other student groups' levels was the biggest educational part of the course: like many designers the more they designed game levels the less they actually noticed how others would and could play them. This designer versus player divide was brought home to them as soon as they played the levels of other students. For navigation, general feedback and reward systems are the first to go when the designer runs out of time or becomes so involved in the creation they forget about the user experience of players who do not have inside design knowledge of how the game is supposed to be played.

As a teacher, what concerns me most about using a game engine (and we have created in commercial games and game engines such as *Neverwinter Nights*, *Torque*, *Unreal Tournament*, *Warcraft III*, *Morrowind*, and *Half-Life 2/Source)*, is how students let the typical game scenarios constrain the interaction scenarios of the games they wished to design. It was usually quite difficult for them to conceptualize novel and appropriate forms of interaction that were both engaging and educational in relation to the envisaged game mod, and not to the default game.

What follows are nine examples of the game engines and game levels we used to create games in six to twelve or thirteen week periods. I am sure there are many more ways of designing and evaluating modding in a classroom situation, but I hope this will be interesting and relevant to the way you use or teach games and game mods.

Cultural History and Game Levels: NWN and Magic with Monkeys

At the University of Queensland, from 2005 to 2006, over a hundred undergraduate students in multimedia and information environment degrees were taught an introduction to game design course. Apart from the lectures there was also a design component, using *Warcraft III* or *Neverwinter Nights* (or even *StarCraft*) to build their own game levels. This was only a thirteen-week course (one of four courses) and it predominantly concentrated on game design theory for people who did not study the subject before. While a few of the students had been professional game players, some of the students enrolled in the course without having played computer games.

I won't discuss the many undergraduate projects here, but instead concentrate on a 2006 postgraduate cohort of three students. This project is of interest to me and relevant here because of the issues the students encountered. These included not only the technical aspects of modding, the creative challenges in transferring a descriptive medium (epic novel) to an interactive medium, and in terms of designing and evaluating for different cultural groups.

As one of the students was not Australian but from mainland China, I suggested designing a game around *Journey to the West*, as taken from the 16th Century original Chinese text. The story commenced in Xian, China, but covered a journey of mythical characters along the Silk Route to the borderlands of India. It has been told in many forms and versions across TV, film and games, and translated into many languages. English speakers are probably most familiar with the Japanese TV series *Monkey Magic*, the BBC also dubbed this series, creating a cult classic.

All three students had heard of *Journey to the West* before, although the two Australian students knew it as *Monkey Magic*. The Chinese student also knew both the British-Japanese and Chinese television versions, but saw the Japanese version as an incorrect retelling of the story. The student was able to provide the other two students with accurate information and a translation of the original text to work from. Initially, this student was reluctant to accept that a game engine could accurately portray the cultural nuances of the Chinese version.

Due to the large size of the original book, the students based the level upon a single chapter. Chapter 59 recounted the adventures of the four main characters, Monkey, Pigsy, Sandy and Monk Sanzang as they attempt to cross the Fiery Mountains on their journey west to recover Holy Scriptures for the Tang Emperor. On their way, they must convince the antagonist, Iron Fan Immortal (also known as Raksasi), to lend them her Plantain Fan in order to blow out the fires which block their passage west (*Figure 1*). The game was to focus on the dealings of Monkey, a being possessed of great physical and magical power, as he fights enemies and the elements to reach his goal.

Figure 1; The scene where Monkey encounters Raksasi (Iron Fan Immortal).

The postgraduate group decided to test BioWare's *Neverwinter Nights* (NWN) *Aurora toolset Engine* (with the Diamond pack addition) as a story-making device, and to critique how well *Neverwinter Nights* worked as a modding tool, especially for designing serious games. *NWN* is typically used to create role-playing adventures in the popular *Dungeons & Dragons* style. It featured a tile-based building system, and placed major terrain elements quasi-randomly; the modder could also place smaller objects, such as furniture, trees and signposts, as well as creatures. There was also a scripting language allowing the level designer to define events and creature or items, through various triggers.

NWN had pedigree, of a sort. The game engine had been used by several education institutes, such as MIT (2003), West Nottinghamshire School (2007), and the University of Michigan (2006). Researchers were very interested in the use of this game genre, as it focuses on role-play. The Institute for the Future of the Book (2006) noted:

> For example, the Education Arcade's game, Revolution, teaches American History. The game was created using the *Neverwinter Night*s game engine. However, problems often arise because the actions of characters are often geared towards the violent, and male and female models are not representative of real people. Therefore, rather than focusing on the funding of games, creating a game engine and other game production tools to be made open source and freely distributed would provide an important resource for the non-commercial gaming community.

It is fair to say that these projects all appeared to run into major problems with using *NWN*, but it is also quite possible that they had trouble in portraying historical and literary events and characters as essential parts of an engaging game. Nonetheless, our three students attempted to design their game level using *NWN*, over a very short time period of 12-13 weeks. As they soon discovered, they also ran into *NWN* constraints. For example, in their original proposal, the students said they would use *NWN*'s ability to allow the player to switch between the three main heroes (allowing a broader but more thematic range of experiences and playing styles). The *NWN* mage's ability to possess his familiar (animal companion) could allow character swapping in the game mod. Unfortunately, the coding logistics allowing the players to transform between the main characters were too complex and obscure for the time given.

Certain abilities exhibited by main characters, such as Monkey's ability to morph into 72 different forms, were held back by the limitations of the toolset. While analogues were available (in this case the polymorph spell), they did not allow any leeway in terms of choice of form – five were given, and only five were usable. None of these forms were particularly suitable for the characters or cultural setting. Forms that Monkey actually used during his adventures in the original Chinese novel would have been preferable, such as birds, flies, and other races (as well as the ability to copy specific people). The students had also debated whether it was possible to include Monkey's ability to fly on a small cloud that could move at high speed. This was abandoned due to modeling/importing issues.

In my view, while being able to morph into familiars was a nice touch, being able to transform into or between major characters would be a powerful narrative device. Imagine if the player could suddenly, deliberately, or perhaps randomly change between characters, and that this affects the way the game level appears (such as field of view, lighting, music, shaders), the nature and balance of game mechanics, or perhaps the played history changes dependent on the character.

Other non-playing characters (NPCs) such as an old man, cake seller and woodsman were characters in the original story and also featured in the game (*Figure 2*). They could converse with the player and impart clues and parts of the original story.

119

Figure 2; NPCs could talk to Monkey to advance the story.

There were also issues with how to stage the drama and conflict engagingly as a game. In the game the students altered the dramatic events from attacking monsters to ambushing bandits. Individually, bandits were relatively weak, and until they were in groups of eight or more, they were no great challenge. Still, they were far from helpless, using ambush tactics, and sneaking while patrolling, inducing the player to slow down and scan the environment, rather than risk running blindly into traps. Dying bandits also dropped healing potions that Monkey could pick up, these potions were necessary to combat the Iron Fan Immortal, the villain of the adventure. Still, fighting bandits was optional, and a careful player could sneak around potential ambushers.

Exploration in the level was also useful for gaining bonus items, including skill and armor increasing equipment, special potions (speed, bark-skin, strength and dexterity), as well as higher quality healing potions. The overall level was very large, and, interestingly, while wide expanses of wilderness appeared to convey the loneliness of the desert and the epic nature of the journey; participants in the evaluation did not complain that it detracted from their goals. Certain areas, for instance the temple on Little Mount Sumeru (*Figure 3*, left), were held in high regard by play testers; mainly for the use of the bamboo (one tester described the ambiance as "romantic" and many others listed it as their favorite area).

Figure 3; The romantic settings in this level were remarked upon by play-testers.

The difficulties associated with importing custom content were numerous, and so the students were forced to work with what content was available to them. The students were fortunate insofar as the desert terrain type, in which the story was primarily set, contained pseudo-Eastern architecture, somewhere between Middle Eastern and Asiatic in style (*Figure 4*). This fitted their goal somewhat, as the group agreed that culture in the southwest of China at that time was influenced by Indian and other powers from further west.

Still, the differences between Tang Dynasty temple architecture and the default *NWN* temple are obvious to those who know what to look for. So it was fortunate that the students had chosen the story of the Fiery Mountains as the inspiration for the game. By using a story set in mostly desert terrain and wilderness areas such as mountains, the students avoided the difficulties associated with creating towns and civilization, namely the almost total lack of Eastern architecture inside *NWN*.

Figure 4; The NWN Toolset temple (left) and (right) temple as used in the game.

The game also lacked Chinese style clothes, placeables (e.g. furniture), armor and weapons. Tile sets in the *Aurora Toolset* were often incompatible with one another; which prevented terrain type crossovers and content sharing. The *Community Expansion Package* (CEP) provided clothing, placeable items and weapon variants that had obviously been designed for use with a Japanese setting, and many of these were adopted for use in the project; including a kimono, Sandy's moon-staff, rush mats, bamboo placeables, amongst others.

There were serious technical issues in constructing the game levels. The *NWN* game engine was unreliable and unpredictable when used for modding, especially when adding hak packs. The *Neverwinter Nights - BioWare* site offered tutorials and forums as a support network but as with other games, the company was preparing for a new release and stopped supporting the (then) current version, the web forum emptied and tutorials were four years old and not updated. Official *BioWare* walkthroughs were complex for budding game designers, and community created tutorials were often incomplete, incorrect or out of date (although this may have improved with the release of *Neverwinter Nights 2*).

Support for the importing of custom content was also very limited. Additional content, while created, was universally rejected by the system, despite remakes, import-procedural changes and multiple tutorial assistances. The models that were produced were limited to clothes (robes) due to time restrictions, but would eventually have included weaponry, and, importantly, architecture. To create new content, an entire expansion package could be devoted to creating the new tile sets, placeables, body-types, and items that would be required – far too much for the casual builder to implement without significant assistance.

For example, one of the most glaring problems with using *NWN* was the complete lack of Asiatic body forms, especially for facial features. For characters such as Pigsy (who requires a monstrous face) this was not so much of an issue; however Monkey, Monk Sanzang and Sandy, not to mention the various NPC adversaries and bystanders this was an issue. The primary villain, Iron Fan Immortal (Raksasi), was fortunate in receiving a head with a hairstyle reminiscent of Asian influence, and vaguely Asiatic features, however she was the only one among an overwhelming majority of European featured character models. The *Community Expansion Package* (CEP) included a head designed for use in a Japanese setting; however the modeling of the face was not of suitable high resolution, and was therefore discarded.

When the game level design was completed, fourteen testers were consulted, and their responses recorded in both qualitative and quantitative forms. These final tests were done using a range of players, from seven year-olds to university students, including experienced gamers and people who have no experience with games at all. The students also had a fair mix of gender and ethnicity (including a large component of Chinese students) amongst the testers. The latter were the most enthusiastic about the game, as all had grown up with the story and claimed to know it well. However, the Chinese testers were more likely to skip dialogue, as they felt that they already knew what was being said.

While in the original *Journey to the West* story the information is passed on in conversation, the play-testing showed that most players of the game would prefer to just exit the conversations at the earliest opportunity. The Chinese play-testers in particular moved through the level generally ignoring the conversations, noting on their feedback forms that they knew the story very well already and would play on that knowledge alone, while the western play-testers scrolled through the conversations and some even killed the NPCs rather than converse with them, and thus received no journal entry. The students did not think many play-testers even viewed the journal. For example, none of the seven Chinese participants completely read the story introduction before starting to play the game.

There were also cultural differences in judgment on the game characters. One Chinese participant complained that Monkey's power and skills/ abilities were too limited and too weak, far below expectations. The other Chinese participants were also the most vocally critical about the portrayal of Monkey's character. Nearly all said that he was too weak, compared to his adversaries. The other non-Chinese testers did not find this to be an issue. For example, one non-Chinese participant declared it was a "lovely story", and "the character is very creative and special".

A majority of testers felt that the action was also well paced. However, a hidden sublevel designed by the students, the Bandit Hideout, was rarely found by players even though it was not particularly well hidden. Students can often underestimate how different it is to navigate and wayfind in games compared to the real world. Studies have shown that people typically do not look around in web-based virtual environments, that is, unless they have to. They typically "walk" straight ahead, and as peripheral vision in a virtual environment is typically much more restricted, and as they are virtually gliding in a set path rather than bouncing around (which is what we do when we walk in the virtual world), the surrounding parts of these environments are not perceived and not remembered.

The students also learnt the difficulties of including prescriptive knowledge (reading journal entries) with an action-orientated game, and especially for players who thought they already knew the story. For example, the Chinese testers all said that they would be interested to play such a game, and were very enthusiastic to play, before they had been introduced to it. Yet during play they were prone to skip dialogue, and run headlong into fights expecting a hands-down victory, and became disappointed when they were forced to retreat. In hindsight the students also believed that the intro and outro movies were useless for a similar reason, as most players only watched them once and then clicked through the cutscenes to get to the game play.

I would also have suggested different ways of modifying the game and the storyline. While the journal entries were useful, the illustrations (screenshots) that appeared while different parts of the level were loading could have been used to display historical background information. For the journal entries were easily ignored, detracted from the rest of the screen, and were hard to read. The scripting would also have been helped by tools such as *ScriptEase*. Boundaries and transition points or portals were also not integrated into the game. The 'slash and hack' game genre also prevented the students from creatively matching player interaction to dramatic events in the original story.

I believe a stronger emphasis on character design rather than on setting design is important when portraying cultural or historic information inside a game. For instance, the play-testers who knew the *Journey to the West* story (generally the film or comic versions) complained that Monkey was not powerful enough and that Pigsy was too powerful. These arguments of character portrayal were based upon Monkey's portrayal as literally the 'Equal of Heaven' in the original story; he had almost limitless power.

In terms of level design, the student group should have created a test level earlier in the game design course, as it would have helped them to visualize how to populate areas more realistically. They also observed they saw another issue: in the original epic, Monkey and his band only battle when it is necessary, while in the game the player gains experience points as a result of their battles. Designing a graphical overview of the game level, with rewards and punishments (or constraints and affordances) would have helped them balance out the components and mechanics of gameplay in a more thematically appropriate way.

The play testing issues listed by the students in their final reports were to a certain extent surmountable, and they could be better resolved by play testing earlier in the piece and by catering for a wider range of playing styles and domain knowledge. For example, by designing mechanisms that simply allowed those players (who already knew the story) to skip the historical details and character introductions. Similarly, for the less culturally experienced players, more details regarding the story could be added to the introduction in a preferably interactive manner to enhance greater player engagement.

The students realized that cyclical testing as a continual iterative process would have aided the production of their game considerably. While the group tested areas as they were made, it would perhaps have been more beneficial to play-test using outsiders. For example, there was some unexpected play tester behavior, one participant did not appear to enjoy encountering the enemies and tried hard to avoid them – but the students had not set up tools to observe and analyze such unusual behavior.

So *NWN* was not an ideal modding tool either for this game or for most historical reconstructions; it lacked preset content and ease-of-use functionality. As the toolset was largely designed for producing adventures set in the *Dungeons and Dragons* world of Faerun (largely Western influenced), it was difficult to create anything other than *D & D* without a great deal of time and effort.

Another danger for new but enthusiastic modders is that commercial game genres may restrict rather than inspire designers to use meaningfully appropriate interaction. The evaluation found a fascinating variety of cultural assumptions by players as to the supposed authenticity of the story. Game-based collaborative learning has more to offer virtual heritage and cultural learning than simply modifying single player adventure games. In Journey to the West, which seems to have at least four different cultural retellings, the multivalency itself could have become a game feature, involving various players, NPCs and perhaps to adjudicate, an experienced player, local, or a teacher, acting as guide, instructor or referee (*NWN* allows a Dungeon master). Players may have to share their knowledge, work out collaboratively which is or is not authentic, and try to stop rivals from unraveling the truth. If game level editors allowed designers to create character transformations this may also be an interesting dramaturgical device.

Spirit Narratives: Unreal ghosting in Megalithic Maltese Temples

Another game mod project was a mod in the sense it was created using *Unreal Tournament 2004*, but the content was mostly created by the student level designer. The project group consisted of third year university students enrolled in multimedia and information environments degrees, and the course was a multimedia design project, with an external client. The initial design problem I suggested they look at was whether low-cost game environments with thematic interaction could be developed to convey impressions of an archaeological site as it may have been inhabited. Their client was Bernadette Flynn, who taught film studies at Griffith University (also in Queensland). She was starting a PhD and was very interested in performance and spatial issues in game design. Bernadette suggested a visualization of a world heritage site in Malta. Malta has some of the oldest stone temples in the world, but we know very little of the rituals that went on inside them.

From the illustrations and measured drawings that Bernadette gave the students, they were able to create a 3D model and transport it to the editor that can be used to create *Unreal Tournament* levels. The students created small fires for rituals, and ways of moving sacred items from one special place to another. They also discovered they could add videos of real people inside the level as guides (*Figure 5*). However the quality of these videos was vague, almost ghostly, so we decided to change the idea of guides into more spiritual inhabitants. They could be triggered by the movement or correct actions of the player, or they could be triggered to start their own rituals at pre-set times

Figure 5; An early stage of the Maltese temple prototype before texturing was completed.

While the game level was comparatively simple (*Figure 5*), it allowed
Bernadette to visualize how she would create her own highly immersive
and interactive visualization of Mnajdra, (which she would later design and
evaluate at iCinema UNSW, using Virtools VR software). Bernadette also
presented the student work to help convey her own design ideas and theories
at a conference in Malta itself, so as a thirteen-week prototype I believe this
project succeeded.

Not a Mod but Mod-worthy: Unreal Heart beating Terror with a Plastic Sword

I had an issue. I had just bought a head mounted display (HMD) with a
small research grant, an eMagin z800 3D visor. The resolution was a (then)
respectable 800 by 600 pixels. It promised head tracking and an interesting
alternative to using a computer screen, at a relatively affordable price. We
connected it up to *Unreal Tournament* and *Half-Life 2* and apart from some
driver problems you gained some idea of an immersive display. There was
however one big issue; the lag. If I turned my head around while inside a
computer game the game environment rotated the point of view for me
about half a second after I turned my head! Had I bought an expensive white
elephant? Could we still use this equipment for game design projects?

126

What about a horror game? It felt very creepy to turn your head around inside
say *Half-life 2* and then slowly, slowly would the camera turn. Obviously
the head tracking was too ponderous for a typical first person shooter, but
what about a horror game? The delay might actually add to the atmospheric
uncanniness of a claustrophobic horror game. Can the constraints of the
HMD be overcome through simple game design, and, (back to my perennial
research interest), can this game use historical knowledge and physical
computing (biofeedback etc.) in an interesting and engaging way?

A student team of four wanted to use the HMD along with biofeedback.
So I suggested recreating the legend of the Minotaur of the Labyrinth. The
level would be dark and claustrophobic, the tunnels of the hypothetical
Labyrinth. The goal would be (as Theseus), to find and kill the Minotaur (a
simple goal in itself but this was just a test case). I suggested that as the player
neared the Minotaur (who could be spawned randomly, near the center of the
Labyrinth), spooky music could increase in volume. That however was not the
most atmospheric element. As the player approached the unseen monster, the
volume of the combined heartbeats (and / or GSR turned into heart beating
sounds) would likewise increase. The player, with the HMD, would also have
a plastic sword (that covered the 3D joystick). The movement and position of

the plastic sword would be fed into the game level.

Another idea I had was not taken up by the students, but is something I hope to try out in the near future. Imagine yourself in an underground labyrinth. The light is bad, the corridor is crowded, but as you get to the end of a passageway you might feel the air from the tunnel at right angles to the tunnel you came from. Thanks to the HMD, we could track the position and orientation of the player's head. I thought we could take four fans, place them around the player, and they would blow air on the play in relation to the virtual position of the tunnels. According to ANZAC veterans, who were hidden by locals during World War II, the herbs and flowers on the island of Crete are highly scented and evocative. With this in mind, I also hoped to place small baskets of herbs in front of the fans so the moving air would be scented.

Two students researched issues in biofeedback; the third researched and designed the level, the fourth researched Greek/Cretan mythology and archaeology. The students create a brief for their level in which they wrote their aim was to develop a game style level and test the use of peripherals (HMD, 3D joystick, and biofeedback) as connected to the game. They would evaluate user response in terms of immersion, enjoyment, and usability factors.

I asked British archaeologists for permission to use their panoramas of Knossos for the project, and luckily they agreed. Legend had it that the Labyrinth was the maze under the palace of Knossos in Crete. Although there is debate over the semantic distinctions between a labyrinth (linear-path) and a maze (multiple paths), writers tend to conflate the two, so I will do so here. The one under Knossos appears to have been a labyrinth but the one created by Daedalus was probably a maze as myths claimed it was so hard to find the way out that even Daedalus would have trouble escaping it. Thus the bigger issue for us was that the bronze-age labyrinth under Knossos was not big enough or complex enough to be the mythical Labyrinth, while Crete has other more complex natural and artificial mazes. Given this archaeological uncertainty over where or what the Labyrinth was, the students decided to design a more hypothetical level in order to create a more horror-inducing atmosphere.

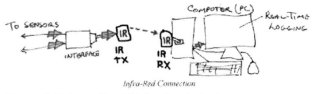

Figure 6; Schematic of Biofeedback device.

This was to be a two-semester (two x thirteen weeks) project. In the first semester the students created the Level (Minoan labyrinth) and the Minotaur. They visited a psychologist experienced in biofeedback who suggested ways of designing biofeedback equipment that did not pose a danger to participants, and with that knowledge they custom-built a simple GSR (galvanic skin response) biofeedback device and demonstrated it working at the end of semester presentation (*Figure 6*). However, they did not continue the project in semester 2, so I will have to wait until I find another team willing to take on this project.

Unreal Projection

Can 3D spatial projection enhance a sense of spatial presence and atmosphere?

When evaluating archaeology students and visualization experts in 2004, I had found that people typically move forward rather than walk around when navigating web-based virtual environments on a PC, so I wanted to see how peripheral projection may engage and encourage people to better explore their environment. In 2005 I supervised a student project where my digital reconstruction of a Mayan city, Palenque, was ported to a game engine.

For this project we built a special environment where the game was projected onto a large specially constructed black book consisting of three walls and a ceiling roughly 2.4 meters in each direction (*Figure 6*). The player stood just in front of this box, looking inside it. A projector projected the game environment onto a curved mirror that in turn reflected the game back onto the back and side walls and ceiling in front of the player.

Figure 7; The Lightning stick (left) and Xibalba (right).

The player could navigate with a 3D joystick; their task was to find the Mayan version of the underworld, Xibalba. The first task for the player was to find the shaman, and take their magical lightning stick (*Figure 7*). With the lightning stick in their hand, they were then instructed to find the Mayan Ball Court (where the Mayans played their ritual ball game, and which featured in their Creation myth stories). When the player found the Ball court and pointed the magical lightning stick at it, lightning zapped across the screen causing the Ball court to split open and the player would fall into the opening hole and find themselves dispatched to Xibalba (which was modeled on the description found in the Mayan book, *The Popol Vuh*).

One interesting discovery of this project was the immersive aspect of projection that catered for peripheral vision. When people are surrounded by a large game space in three dimensions that is bigger than they are, and when they interact by standing and moving (we used sensor pads to allow people to move by physically walking onto the mat), the scale of the place and the embodiment of the visitor begins to develop into an entirely new perspective.

The *UT2004* game engine allowed quick and easy use of current models (including avatars and flying birds), was significantly quicker than the original environment I created using *Adobe Atmosphere*, provided easy ways to add a dynamic compass and other navigation cues, and could project via several cameras at once (it has been used to run in a CAVE). Despite *UT2004* being used for many projects, coding could be laborious, it was not (at the time) easy to port across platforms, and it is unclear how much of the project could run in *UT3* (although I think it can be ported, I have not yet had time to try!)

129

Figure 8; Room Projection of Palenque in UT 2004 (picture on left courtesy of Paul Bourke).

The mirror projection was based on the work of Paul Bourke, a visualization expert, who visited us this year with his mirror projection inside an inflatable dome setup (*Figure 9*). He creates projections for planetariums, artists, and the military; and by using semi-spherical mirrors and complex image warping code, he can avoid expensive fish eye lens while creating a peripheral and spatially rich experience for one or more viewers.

Figure 9; Paul Bourke's portable inflatable dome (left) and inside (right).

Extending Paul Bourke's projection work of panoramas and movies to interactive real-time rendering engines allowed another student to develop Open GL code for calibration of mirror projection onto curved or warped or distorted surfaces. The masters student (Charles Henden) developed the warping mesh and a graphic user interface (GUI) so game designers can easily can move dots on the screen to warp the mesh so that a game (in this case *UT2004*) projects accurately onto curved and 3D surfaces. The project is now finished and part of the open source ongoing *CAVE UT* project hosted by *http://publicvr.org.*

Burnout and Torque: Create a Tent for Car-Racing Games

The next project was actually two projects, but with the same student team. Inspired by Paul Bourke's work on low-cost surround projection methods, they decided to create game environments where the player was not shutoff from the audience. For computer games are typically on flat screens obscured from a wider audience. Can we include the audience and enhance spatial presence? By creating wraparound screens and tents, the students hoped to create a more dramatic and immersive environment which allowed an audience to also share part of the spectacle.

So the students sewed together panels for a low cost dome (*Figure 10*). Sound-speaker lounges are set up for the player; games are projected onto a 60 cm diameter chromed mirror that projects onto the inside of the dome. The game they used was *Burnout*, and they also acquired a specialist car racing steering wheel and pedal set. The chair was a relatively inexpensive commercially available peripheral specially designed for computer games; sound and vibrations were fed into it from the computer.

The spatial size and encompassing field of view engaged the player, and hid external distractions. The game itself had screen view options that were adequate for the screen, so no additional coding was required. The project received a great deal of attention from staff and students while being built and when exhibited, it was particularly immersive thanks to the way it engaged peripheral vision. I apologize for the low quality photos, the room was deliberately dark for the sake of immersion but the camera we had available at the time had trouble coping with the low light conditions.

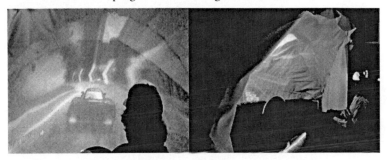

Figure 10; A canvas projection screen for car racing.

For their other project the students created a low-cost tent-like installation (*Figure 11*). The students used and adapted a game level demonstration in the *Torque* game engine. Various configurations were built that incorporated force feedback in the steering, and force feedback into the chair, for car racing and collision-based games such as the *Torque* demo. A digital massage chair was placed under a truck seat the students found on a rubbish heap. They created code that sent the displacement of the car in the *Torque* game demo level to the massage chair so that the truck seat the player sat on would shake them in relationship to the landscape.

Figure 11; A surround environment for car racing

We found on play-testing with the gently curved projection screen that a curved mirror and recalibrated screen warping was not needed to engage peripheral vision and a sense of immersion. A second monitor outside the tent allowed an audience to watch. Ideally another student would have created a camera tracked table that recorded audience gestures so that they could virtually lift landscape objects and place them in the way of the player's car. Not surprisingly, this was too ambitious an add-on. There were however LED lights (visible in the upper right picture in *Figure 11*). Data could be sent to these LED lights from the player's biofeedback and reveal the player's stress levels to the audience.

Source: Zombies Who Feed on Fear

We had a problem. Computer game players have physiological reactions to games that are not incorporated into the game due to the limited Windows and mouse/joystick interface devices. Is it possible to use biofeedback cheaply and accurately in a game that adds to enjoyment even if the player does not directly control or even realize biofeedback is being used? Also, could this be used as an indirect evaluation method?

The solution we arrived at was to create a socket between a cheap biosensor device and a game that suits the genre and setting, (in this case a horror zombie level). We bought the meditational game *Wild Divine*, and modified the interface so that it would work with the *Half Life 2*: source game engine (Dekker and Champion, 2007). The student chose an existing game level, *Ravensholm*, and added some invisible triggers into the level. Depending on the galvanic skin response and heartbeat, the code would dynamically change the AI, the music, the Field of View, the graphic shaders, and other elements (such

Figure 12. Biofeedback attached to Half-Life 2 Source game engine.

as shaking the camera) according to how calm, stressed or bored the player was. In order words, the more stressed or scared you got, the scarier became the zombies, the lighting, the music, and the cinematic effect (*Figure 12*).

The honours students tested 14 people, via a placebo interface and the real biofed game. Their subjective recall was measured, they were video-recorded, and their physiological state (as recorded by the Wild Divine sensor) was tracked against what actually happened in-game. We found changes in the music to be the most dramatic. The players generally knew which one was the biofeedback level, but they did not try or learn how to control the game effects through the biofeedback.

Using indirect biofeedback has several advantages. You can create a great sense of uncanniness and atmosphere, the dramatic elements can be heightened, and the vague or inaccurate problems of direct biofeedback are avoided. That said, this was just a prototype to see if the mechanics were sound, I would like to test this further, not in zombie games, but in meditational spaces, where the calmer the player, the more things happen.

Is it possible to add to gameplay through subconscious and automatic player reaction? After all, the mouse and keyboard are very constrained and mechanical forms of human input. If a game (and longer term, a virtual heritage environment) could automatically and dynamically react to the instinctive reactions and physiological state of the player, it could increase the frequency or intensity of elements that most excite (or calm) the player.

While there is extensive work using Virtual Reality to control phobias, there is still little research on the user-reactive aesthetics of gameplay. This project demonstrated via a game mod that low cost biofeedback can be introduced into a virtual environment for aesthetic reasons, for atmospheric augmentation and to emphasize key dramatic moments and elements. These devices and effects may allow us to track player engagement, but they can also dynamically adjust the content to make it more engaging, and hence more memorable.

Mummies in Morrowind: Embedded Cognitive Artifacts

Can we create engaging experiences that also educate? Can players learn about history or archaeology in an interesting and not violent-focused way? Can the interface be a learning tool?

The journal and map entries of games could be incorporated into educational puzzles and quests, but these have not yet been fully developed, as far as I know, by educationalists. In my teaching and research I have tried to approach these problems by thematically constraining the player, and by augmenting graphic gameplay with textual diaries using the built in tools of game editors. This use of journals, diaries and maps I call external cognitive artifacts. If these external cognitive artifacts are initially fragmented, and can be augmented dynamically by the player's intentions and activities, they may also act as evaluation devices.

Figure 13; Elder Scrolls III: Morrowind and the Egyptian Temple of the Gods.

How can we use maps as external cognitive artifacts? A third year student group decided to use the level editor in *Elder Scrolls III: Morrowind* to create an interactive Egyptian archaeology project. Even in 2006, *Morrowind* was relatively old, and only cost around 10 Australian dollars to purchase. The students quickly developed a fictional Egyptian temple (*Figure 13*), with textual entries giving the player information on how to recreate the powers of individual Egyptian gods. As they read the hieroglyphs, these hieroglyphs would transfer to their inventory map, giving them certain god-like powers.

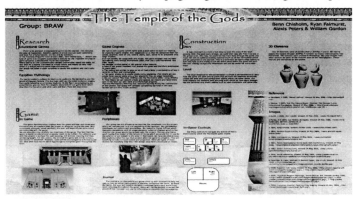

Figure 14; The concept and design was followed closely by the final game level.

To ensure the player did not dawdle, the students called up the skeleton guards in the original game. They also kept the *Morrowind* sword for the player, which was not particularly appropriate! The conflict between allowing people time to reflect, and also creating a sense of urgency to heighten immersion, is a continual dilemma for me. I should also note in passing that the skeletons were not at all like mummies, and were really an entertainment device. However, the speed with which the students designed and ported the 3D models, the care in which they developed their story (*Figure 15*), and their escalating interest in Egyptian archaeology and mythology, was reward in itself.

Marco Polo and the Cultural Turing Test

It has been noted that culture is improvised and transformative, for social rules are not set instructions like chess. Experiencing a virtual environment may be enhanced if the social rules and cultural artifacts can be modified. However, there are two aspects to this; the social world as lived by people inside the 'world', and the perceived social world projected into the environment as seen by people outside that 'world'.

Ideally, virtual environments should afford the "inner" or etic viewpoint. Hodder (1986: 23) argued that "ritual regulates the relationship between people and environment", and that meaning is related to function. Tilley (1999: 29) agreed, "Rituals not only say something, they do something." Childe (1956) stated that myths are actually important; they are instructions to do rational things, only the instructions often carry some additional irrational steps.

135

Given that when we travel to other real and virtual places, we don't tend to engage in local rituals or be instructed by local mythological beliefs, how can we visit, appreciate and enjoy another culture? Other visitors from our own culture will almost certainly distract from the contextually situated embedded and embodied cultural experience. A premise that visitors require other real people in the virtual environment in order to feel a sense of local cultural presence is thus unsubstantiated and highly problematic.

However, it occurred to me that we could solve the social presence problem (not "hell is other people", but "tourism is to be surrounded by like-minded people"), and the believable agents problem (scripted bots in games are seldom convincingly human-like in their apparent intelligence). We could design a situation where the authenticity of the player (and not the NPCs) is called into question (*Figure 15*). By asking users to imitate inhabitants and avoid detection (by agents or other users), we are introducing challenging game elements while at the same time allowing them to learn contextually relevant behavior and local knowledge.

In order to satisfy the NPCs that the player is a "local", the player has to satisfy questions and perform like the actual local characters (the scripted NPCs). Hence the player has to observe and mimic these artificial agents, for fear of being discovered. I have called this a cultural Turing test, but in fact it is a reversal of the Turing test where a questioner has to determine from written answers if the writer is a human or a computer. Here the computer

Figure 15; UT2004 bot (NPC) in Palenque reconstruction.

(through the artificial characters) is trying to determine if the human player is sufficiently artificial character-like. A changing mix of scripted characters and real world users adds a form of mystery and engagement, and helps ensure a reasonable level of challenge persists after the initial learning period.

Combining ideas from role-playing and spy games, a promising option where people learn about rituals is to design a multi-user virtual environment game where the task is to imitate local inhabitants' behavior and dialogue in order to move up the social ladder without being caught (by scripted agents or by other users). There could be a mix of scripted characters and other real-world users, all are trying to detect and catch out inappropriate behavior, interaction or dialogue (inappropriate in terms of space, time, or social encounter). Progression could be achieved by advancing through a social hierarchy that in return offers more power and increased freedom and enhanced interactivity.

I believe this scenario addresses some of the problems of social presence and cultural presence. On the one hand, multi-user environments are inherently engaging; on the other hand, we may wish to restrict users' contextual interaction and dialogue so that they learn about the local culture and not use the setting as a mere chat room. Such a scenario requires a 'believably' intelligent Artificial Intelligence that appears to have agency, agon (competition), and alterity (sense of otherness). However, as a sort of cultural Turing test, this scenario may allow the integration of historical fact, cultural behaviors, embedded multiple users, and goal based motivation that relies on acquiring contextually appropriate cultural knowledge, not destroying it.

While the Palenque environment in *Unreal Tournament* had default bots and wildlife, with a student group I decided to develop a new environment in the *Half-Life 2*: Source engine. The game scenario was the return of Marco Polo to Italy from China about twenty four years after he had left. In real life, the bearded and much changed Marco Polo was not recognized by his family on his return from China, and many people refused to believe his stories. Once they eventually did recognize and accept him as being Marco Polo, he was still described as ""the man of a million lies" (Wood, 1995). We still don't know today if he visited China and was appointed as governor by the Emperor, or merely recounted stories he heard from traders while he was in Persia.

Given this interesting background, we imagined a hypothetical situation where an agent from Emperor Khan attempts to reach Italy before Marco Polo, impersonate him, and try infiltrate the local aristocracy to steal their cultural artifacts and scientific knowledge (the Emperor had apparently wanted Marco Polo to send him back wise men from Italy). With this scenario, and using bots that operated on Bayesian logic, the game engine could test the player's cultural knowledge, and track the player's spatial orientation and location, and ability to observe and mimic local knowledge in order to convince them he was actually Marco Polo.

So here lies the challenge: could this cultural Turing test idea be used convincingly in a serious game? Could the player learn enough inside information about social roles, positions and identities through genuine extrapolation, and not just by random guessing? Could we design a game level with a suitable historical setting and an imposter interaction method that created a suitable stealth learning situation (where players learn authentically but in an entertaining way without realizing it?)

In thirteen weeks, with four undergraduate students and a programmer, the answer, was no. This was for me the most unresolved and frustrating project.

I had given the students too much to think about and too difficult a scene to model. The programming student created versions of Bayesian AI which at the last moment would not work with the game level. The game level itself was unresolved, partly because the *Half Life 2* game editor was not easy software to master quickly. And the setting we had chosen, a Venetian palace which Marco Polo returned to; was too difficult to model because those buildings were replaced after he died with the famous buildings of Venice that we see today, thus I found no suitable description or drawings of the Marco Polo-era buildings. And only a few of the design ideas were in place. We had investigated deception detection methods; biofeedback and eye tracking could help give an idea of the stress of the player. Response times to questions and the task performance of the avatar could also indicate uncertainty of knowledge, but these were all crude detection methods.

More than eight years ago I was shown fascinating software where the game character (your avatar) automatically captures and portrays your facial expressions captured in real-time from a web camera of you the player, but I am still waiting for it to be sold and made available to developers. Now, as I write this chapter, there are new and exciting ways of interacting with games and with characters inside games. *Skyrim* on the Xbox Kinect allows you to use various voice commands with characters, but to edit game levels

you require the PC version, not the Xbox version. The promised *Elder Scrolls* MMORPG may allow level editing but if it exists, it is likely to be limited. Commercial biofeedback software and the middleware that some of my ex-students have recently developed may also help us track player responses, and game AI is advancing, but this project requires a great deal of modding, socket programming, and sheer elbow grease. So why mention this project? Not just so someone with adequate resources is inspired to pick it up, but to give at least one example of how intricate and sophisticated the theory and level design of a game mod can be, and sometimes has to be.

Creative Uses of Mods in the Classroom

I tried to compress this chapter as much as I possibly could, and hope you have found a few ideas from the above paragraphs that you might wish to question, extend and play around with. I have a few other ideas for teaching or designing with game mods, and I will mention them in passing.

As a simple but potentially time-consuming exercise, it could be interesting to see what students might learn through reverse engineering. Free 3D software such as *Blender* often provides open source film projects. The 3D assets were used to make digital films, but as the actual digital creative content is also often made available, the students could be asked to try to add or subtract the provided assets, scripts or effects to see what was done (see for example, *http:// orange.blender.org/*).

The academic Thomas Malone wrote several papers in the early 1980s on the elements that made games successful. He would remove or add game elements piece by piece to see if they were still engaging. In a similar fashion, with demo levels provided by game engines, you could ask the students to add and remove game elements to see which ones are necessary and sufficient, or superfluous.

A potentially simple approach would be to keep the default game level, but change the interaction or interface. I described the *Unreal Palenque* game mod where the default *UT* navigation interface could be adapted into a schematic Mayan calendar. I also mentioned some game environments were basically current game levels but projected onto custom-built surround screens. With game engine one can create not only architectural models but also large-scale landscape visualizations. We could import screenshots or maybe even 3D models from *Google Earth*, and panoramas from *Street view* or similiar programs, then project them around people, onto walls or objects.

Possibly one could create an entirely new way of looking at that game, or show the relationship between the game and the wider environment? With some games, (such as with *Black and White*), one could incorporate real-time data, such as weather conditions data mined from the internet, hand puppets, or real-time live video footage of actors (Gillam and Jacobson, 2012).

Another idea would be to challenge the students to change the sense of agency. One of the most low-key yet conceptually interesting games I have seen designed by an academic is *Space Refugees* by Zach Whalen. It is a simple game created in *Flash*, and appears at first glance to be a *Space Invaders!* homage. Well it is homage in a way, but a reflective one. Instead of shooting the alien spacecraft, you yourself are an alien in the spacecraft, trying to find sanctuary after your planet is destroyed. Instead of finding sanctuary, you get to see all the survivors of your race shot down around you as you all try to land. You can try to escape the gunfire from the ground but you yourself cannot fire back.

I won't argue whether it is a mod or not, as one can say it is parodying *Space Invaders!* It is indisputably a completely separate game. However, just like *September 12,* designed by newsgaming (which is pretty clearly a standalone game), it asks the player to review their conventional understanding by placing themselves in the position of innocent victim (*Space Refugees*) or would-be hero who is actually making the inescapable tragedy even worse (September 12).

Now that *Portal 2* features a game level editor (Gilbert, 2011), I think an interesting project would be to see if we can create a game which creates portals not only in space and orientation (like *Portal 1* and *2*), but also in time. Just as the physics surrounding the player somehow works across portals, enabling the player to solve various puzzles, perhaps the physics could change into magic and mythical beliefs depending on which space and time continuum one was on. Would this encourage students to learn about earlier ideas of nature and science? I am not sure. Definitely this is highly ambitious, but perhaps, one day, possible!

Lessons Learnt

I quickly and continually learnt a very simple lesson. When you are teaching game design in ten or twelve weeks, don't let any gung-ho students build a game engine from scratch. As part of one class I supervised a small breakaway group (of two!) undergraduate students as they built a complete real-time rendering engine for their 2D game design, in ten weeks. So they were coding the real-time rendering engine and then designing the game level. Not surprisingly, the game level completion rate suffered, even if the game engine and the game worked, their crafty ideas for mutually dependent gameplay never had time to be revealed. It was however a notable example of the ambitiousness of those starting out for the first time, and just like the more modest game design proposals of other less program-orientated students, the usability, general navigation, and feedback systems all suffered to such an extent that would-be players required extensive instruction and hands-on examples from the designers themselves.

Perhaps that is why the trailer video to the first *Portal* game was so remarkable, it created huge excitement in potential players, giving them a very clear idea of how the game could be played as an enjoyable (and yet terrifying) learning experience, and simultaneously employed reverse psychology: defying players to actually survive. I see *Portal* as an excellent example of a successful virtual learning environment, both entertaining and edifying.

Creating simple ideas for new forms of interaction well ahead of time can never be stressed enough. Generally I found new game design students came up with rough and also overly ambitious ideas of how the game would look, but did not spend time until the last possible moment on how to design unique, situated interaction. Creating new and stimulating interaction is not easy, and even the most ardent gamer may overlook how difficult it is to design, thinking they want to design like X and Y, only better. Creative interaction is not a simple addition of different mechanics from different games.

Figure 16. Skeletons in the Egyptian game were not so happy with those who tarried.

Another technique I did not use enough in lectures and tutorials was to encourage the students to physically role-play potential game situations. There are also game cards that enable game design itself to be played out, but I personally believe physically getting students to play out moment to moment experiences focuses them not only what the game looks like but how it is experienced.

I think it is pretty clear by now that I am a proponent of getting students to mark and playtest each other's work. I don't think I can ever over-emphasize to students that they need to spend more time on designing simple rather than complex navigation cues. The more expert the gamer, the less likely they are to realize how confused and disorientated the beginner will be when experiencing their game level for the first time. When students have to play and mark the levels of each other group, it becomes apparent to them, but this is at the end of the course, and simply too late. No matter how much they wish to undertake the complex and artistic scene initially, they must be persuaded to create a rough and dirty level so the mechanics can be ironed out first. In my experience, feedback and reward systems are the backbone to an involving game, but typically added in the latter stages, and often missed altogether.

The above game design projects were to help students learn more about the subject of game design, but they had a spinoff benefit, many of the multimedia students became fascinated by the background content, from Mayan archaeology, to Chinese calligraphy, and Homeric myths. And given the short time frame, evaluation was not a major component of these projects. However, I would like to mention some evaluation issues related to the issue of teaching game mod design. I once saw a conference paper presentation where the audience was told that playing a game based on a wartime event, and reading a book on the subject, proved to be a more effective learning experience than reading a book by itself. Hence, games were effective learning tools. How many students, on given two learning tools, will learn less than if given one learning tool? And how many computer game students would tell their lecturer or tutor that they would rather read a book on history than play a game based on the same events?

Evaluators can often inadvertently induce the participant to say what they think the evaluator wants to hear. While qualitative studies can be vague and unconvincing, quantitative studies are seldom randomized, and there is also the danger of experimental bias. Participants are often not representative

of the market segment (they are all too often fellow computing or media students). Likert responses are often lumped together, and the evaluators are too often also the designers. For experimental design, ideally there is a control environment to compare the new treatment against, and neither the evaluator nor the participant should know exactly what the designer wants to find out, nor should either know which level is the control.

Perhaps because of the creative components of level design, the aims of the evaluation are often discovered just before or after the evaluation. One should always determine potential results *before* designing the experiment. For example, what do you want to find out? How can these findings be proven to back up your hypothesis? And even though you might not know what the output will be, what do you predict? It also pays to calibrate test machines before each evaluation, even on the same model of computer (but with different usage); differing frame rates and hard drive speeds can severely affect respondents' results.

One of the greatest features of mods is that the best way to understand them is to test them and build them yourself. When you are choosing technology, I suggest you could ask yourself the following questions;

• Designer friendliness: Does the tool or editor help you construct quickly and efficiently? Here efficiency does not mean how quickly one can create scripts and 3D assets, but how robust, reliable and appropriate it is in a real-time environment. Are the creation tools and workflows self-explanatory and fluid? Does it feature real-time editing?

• Genre Fluidity: Are the game engine and related assets flexible and fluid enough to accommodate and support various genres and differing settings and style of play?

• Extensibility and reliability: Can it scale across different platforms and accommodate different platforms, efficiently and reliably? Lighting changes, computation changes, the ways in which meshes are generated and portrayed changes, and the development machine may be far more powerful than the machine the mod ends up on. How predictable is the end user performance? Can data and formats be easily transferred across different editors and be safely stored?

• Interactivity: can it connect to a variety of peripherals, does the game engine have the ability to incorporate sockets and in general connect with other programs or web browser scripts (if web-based)?

• Evaluation and analysis: Are there specific tools to help you judge the performance, subjective likes and dislikes, and general impressions of playability? For example, can it handle screen capture software without adversely affecting performance?

• Distribution: what are the legal and copyright issues regards design and distribution of the mod?'

I have learnt the above tips only through bitter-sweet experience. And there are many more considerations to keep in mind, especially when teaching classes of students. No matter the plea of the ambitious student, a complex and graphically powerful game is almost certainly going to require more time and skill than what is available. The ways in which teams of students delegate and divide up work will be crucial to the success of the project and should be part of the assessment (if the project is marked). One of the greatest learning components is also involving the students in the play-testing and marking of each other's games.

Including innovation and the ability to turn a game mod into a reflexive design as components of the assessment are also things I wished I had included in the marking criteria from the start. I cannot emphasize enough the difficulty and significance of taking an existing game and modding it in such a way that the limitations of the original game are addressed, questioned and surpassed by the game mod. The more creative the original game, the more difficult it is for eager students to improve on and transcend the original game mechanics, genre and setting. It is difficult, but not impossible, and when it happens, learning has taken place.

References

BBC news (2007). Computer game to boost key skills. [Electronic version]. Retrieved 1 May 2012, from http://news.bbc.co.uk/2/hi/uk_news/education/6254989.stm

Berger, A. (2006). "Neverwinter Nights" in the classroom, *University of Michigan News online article (dated 31 January)*. [Electronic version]. Retrieved 1 May 2012, from http://www1.umn.edu/news/features/2006/UR_83484_REGION1.html

Blender. (n.d.). Blender. [Electronic version]. Retrieved 1 May 2012, from http://www.blender.org/download/resources/

Carbonaro, M., Cutumisu, M., McNaughton, M., Onuczko, C., Roy, T., Schaeffer, J., Szafron, D., Gillis S. & Kratchmer, S. (2005). Interactive Story Writing in the Classroom: Using Computer Games. *DiGRA 2005 Conference: Changing Views – Worlds in Play,* DiGRA Vancouver, Canada. [Electronic version]. Retrieved 1 May 2012, from http://www.digra.org/dl/display_html?chid=http://www.digra.org/dl/db/06276.35222.pdf

Champion, E., Jacobson, J. (2008). Sharing the Magic Circle with Spatially Inclusive Games. *SIGGRAPH* Asia, Singapore, December.

Childe, V.G. (1956). *Piercing Together the Past.* London: Routledge & Kegan.

Dekker, A., & Champion, E. (2007). Please Biofeed the Zombies: Enhancing the Gameplay and Display of a Horror Game Using Biofeedback. Paper presented at the *DiGRA: Situated Play Conference,* Tokyo, 24-

28 September. Retrieved 1 May 2012, from http://www.digra.org/dl/
db/07312.18055.pdf

Gilbert, B. (2011). Portal 2's second DLC is an 'in-game editor,' arrives 'early
next year'. Joystiq. [Electronic version]. Retrieved 5 May 2012, from
http://www.joystiq.com/2011/10/21/portal-2s-second-dlc-is-an-in-
game-editor-arrives-early-nex/

Gillam, R., Jacobson, J. (2012). The Egyptian Oracle; Live Reenactment
in Augmented Reality, High-Tech Heritage: How Are Digital
Technologies Changing Our Views of the Past? Amherst, MA,
USA, May 2-4. [Electronic version]. Retrieved 5 May 2012,
from Henden, C., Champion, E., Muhlberger, R. & Jacobson, J.
(2008). A Surround Display Warp-Mesh Utility to Enhance Player
Engagement. *International Conference on Entertainment Computing,*
September, Pittsburgh, PA.

Hodder, I. (1986). *Reading The Past.* Cambridge: Cambridge University Press.

Institute for the Future of the Book. (2006). *Funding serious games.*
[Electronic version]. Retrieved 1 May 2012, from http://www.
futureofthebook.org/blog/archives/2006/04/funding_serious_
games_1.html

http://publicvr.org/html/EgyptianOracleHTH-abstract.pdf

Jacobson, J. (n.d.). *publicVR,* [Electronic version]. Retrieved 1 May 2012, from
http://publicvr.org/

Jacobson, J. (2003). Using CaveUT to Build Immersive Displays With the
Unreal Tournament Engine and a PC Cluster, *ACM SIGGRAPH
2003 Symposium on Interactive 3D Graphics,* Monterrey, California,
April. Demonstration and short paper. http://publicvr.org/html/
EgyptianOracleHTH-abstract.pdffrom http://publicvr.org/
publications/I3D-2003.pdf

Jenkins, H., Klopfer, E., Squire K. & Tan, P. (2003). Entering the Education
Arcade. *ACM Computers in Entertainment,* 1 (1). 17-17. [Electronic
version]. Retrieved 1 May 2012, from http://dl.acm.org/citation.
cfm?id=950591

King, T. (2006).User-generated future for gaming. *BBC News.* [Electronic
version]. Retrieved 1 May 2012, from http://dl.acm.org/citation.
cfm?id=950591http://news.bbc.co.uk/2/hi/programmes/click_
online/4997036.stm

Kosak, D.F. (2005). *Will Wright Presents Spore...and a New Way to Think About Games.* Game½spy. Retrieved 1 May 2012, from http://www.gamespy.com/articles/595/595975p1.html

Newsgaming. *September 12.* Electronic version]. Retrieved 1 May 2012, from http://www.newsgaming.com/games/index12.htm

Oman, C. M., Howard, I. P., Smith, T., Beall, A. C., Natapoff, A., Zacher, J. E., & Jenkin, H. L. (2003). The role of visual cues in microgravity spatial orientation. In J. Buckey & J. Homick (Eds.). *The Neurolab Spacelab Mission: Neuroscience Research in Space: Results from the STS-90, Neurolab Spacelab Mission* (pp. 69-81). Houston: NASA. [Electronic version]. Retrieved October 17, 2005, from http://www.psych.ucsb.edu/research/recveb/pdfs/neurolab_report.pdf

Tilley, C. (1999). *Metaphor and Material Culture,* Oxford: Blackwell.

Whalen, Z. (n.d.). *Space Refugees.* [Electronic version]. Retrieved 1 May 2012, from http://www.gameology.org/files/videos/refugees.html

Wood, F. (1995). *Did Marco Polo Go to China?* London: Westview.

Yu, A.C. (1977). *The Journey to the West.* Chicago: University of Chicago Press.

Chapter 6

From

Games to Movies:

Machinima

and Modifications

149

Friedrich Kirschner

150

From Games to Movies: Machinima and Modifications

Prof. Friedrich Kirschner,
Hochschule für Schauspielkunst "Ernst-Busch",
Parkaue 25, 10367 Berlin
friedrich@moviesandbox.net

Introduction

The development of machinima and its perceived potential has, on many occasions, been linked to its production tools, underlying technology and distribution methods.

This is due to the shape that machinima related modifications usually take - mainly: they serve as a way of distributing machinima for playback, they change the game assets and visual style, or they are themselves tools for machinima creation. While the process of distributing machinima as a game modification has all but vanished, tool and asset modifications were not only responsible for the growth and original inception of machinima, but represent an essential aspect of it to this date.

The modding community was in place before machinima was common practice. (Lowood, 2008) Its ways of reconstructing video games, as I will argue, led to the emergence and shape of machinima.

In creating tools and workflows for creative misuse of provided technology, the modding community not only changed video games itself, but also moved beyond the idea of user-generated content. It effectively created its own form of creative expression that became machinima. I call this development user-generated process. It constitutes a new quality in user involvement that moves beyond modification and optimization of a given product into the birth of new processes and even new media. To examine machinima's development in relation to the use and implementation of game modifications, let us look at three distinct historical phases: (1) machinima's initial conception within the "Quake Movie" community, (2) machinima's emergence in mainstream media and (3) the current state of machinima production and distribution. I will place particular emphasis on the second phase. It constitutes a time in which there was much discussion about machinima's potential and a strong community with what Marino calls an "Outside In" approach – filmmakers exploring machinima as a new emerging medium, and not primarily interested in the narrative of the video game. (Marino, 2005)

Phase 1: The formative years

The term machinima originated from the "Quake movie" community, a group of people using the games "Quake" (ID software, 1996) and "Quake 2" (ID software, 1997) not for gameplay, but to film movies (Marino, 2004). These early machinima movies relied heavily on user-created programs to change the basic data structures of the games' demo-files. A demo file contained recordings of events and user-input happening during a game. The way in which these first movies were recorded was very performative in nature. Characters were controlled live by the players, and become the basis of this demo file. Cameras and editing were either set up later in a process known as "re-camming", or controlled by commands that would switch the camera to pre-defined positions. The emergence of live-performed Machinima, as in the case of the ILL-Clan's "Larry and Lenny Lumberjack" (ILL Clan, 2000), or the "Bob Block Machinima Show" (Kirschner, Neumann, Scholz 2004) seemed like a natural form emerging from this mode of production. Quake movies made extensive use of user-generated tools to modify the demo files. In the case of one of the most important tools, Keygrip, the creator was well situated within the modding scene:

> "These coding exploits provided a foundation for David "CRT" Wright's influential Keygrip and Keygrip2 programs, which became the most widely-used utilities for editing and other post-production work on machinima movies. Wright was a mod coder known among Quake players for the Rocket Arena series of one-on-one dueling games... " (Lowood, 2005, p.68)

Figure 1; The Bob Block Machinima Show (Kirschner, Neumann, Scholz, 2004)

Another important aspect of these early Machinima works was the way they were distributed and played back. Instead of being packaged as video files, the work was usually distributed as a demo file and played back within a copy of the game itself, on the viewers' own computer. This required that modifications to environments, characters, scripts and textures had to be installed on the computer of the viewer as well. Machinima was effectively presented as a form of game modification. Machinima's potential for transforming the way animated movies were created was readily visible to early practitioners (Kirschner, 2011). This potential was closely related to the early tools, distribution and production processes laid out by key Modifications such as the aforementioned "Keygrip". While the production method was deemed revolutionary and full of potential, the creative choices left to the Machinima producers in terms of characters, textures or animations were often meager. In addition, the games themselves provided no options for creating these types of assets outside of import/export scripts for the content creation tools used in the production of the games themselves.

The community, often lacking access to these programs, used affordable software like Milkshape 3D – a shareware, low-polygon modeling and animation program (Chumbalum Software, 1996) - to modify or create animations and models to import into Quake and other games. Milkshape in particular was well situated in the modding community, with users often providing importers and exporters for a number of games. In Machinima's formative years, the Modding Community went to great lengths to provide tools for user generated content that went above and beyond the infrastructure provided by video-game production companies. For example, the ILL-Clan created software that allowed their Quake 2 characters to have changing textures for the different stages of their mouth movements, allowing real-time lip-syncing of video-game characters. Some of these tools were not initially intended for Machinima purposes, but were nonetheless crucial in its inception. This reliance on community tools and modifications allowed Machinima's unique production process to be established.

Phase 2: Machinima Renaissance

In what Paul Marino dubbed a "Machinima Renaissance" in his book "the Art of Machinima" (Marino, 2004), a new generation of movies shed their video-game-style graphics ties and presented themselves as visually independent animated films that gained significant mainstream exposure. This newly found graphical fidelity came alongside a new generation of video-game technology, which in turn provided a new generation of tools and creative options:

> "The release of new development tools greatly ushered in new approaches to digital filmmaking" (Marino, 2004).

Some of these new games and tools exposed film-recording functionality. Instead of implementing functionality as laid out by the modding community though, most games were straying away from the early production approach of the Quake movie era, instead introducing a scripted approach suited for cut-scene creation and embedding character and camera control into user-generated levels. Notable example games include "the Sims 2" developed by Maxis (2004) and Unreal Tournament 2004 by Epic Games (2004). Many Machinima movies of this "second phase" could be seen as a direct modification of the game itself. As the games used to create movies stepped away from the demo format and provided tools for procedural scripting of characters and cameras, some of the initial embedded potential lost focus - the idea of live performance, for example, became less and less prevalent. Still, Modifications were employed as a means of distribution, sharing of assets and in the form of tool-sets for producing Machinima. Filmmakers were excited about these new games and their possibilities. Prominent Machinima creator Ken Thain, director of the music video "Rebel vs. Thug" (Hanson 2004) summarized this notion in an interview for Machinimag:

> "There is no one faucet of this medium that is not boiling over with possibilities. The real-time playback aspect, the packaged content aspect, the neo-production possibilities, the high speed of technology advancement, etc, etc. - all that gravy" (Thain, in Kirschner, 2004, p.7)

An indicator of how far Machinima had come in this second phase was the inclusion of Machinima categories in major film and animation-festivals (such as the Bitfilm Festival 2003 or the Ottawa International Animation Festival 2006) and the emergence of contests and competitions with significant incentives for filmmakers to participate, such as the 1,000,000 $ Make Something Unreal Contest.

The Make Something Unreal Contest

The Make Something Unreal Contest (2003) was set up by Nvidia and Epic Games with significant resources to reward excellence in mod making in several categories, including Non-Interactive Real Time Movies (NVIDIA Corporation, Epic Games, 2003).

To be eligible for the non-interactive movie category (the name being an indication that the word "Machinima" was still struggling to gain acceptance in the wider gaming community), the final movie had to be a modification running within the game UT2003 (and later, UT2004). This requirement, as much as Machinima's actual inclusion as a category in the contest was a testament to its Game Modification roots as much as a sign of its potential as perceived from a games industry perspective. The contest aimed to highlight the functionality and ease of use of the then latest Unreal Tournament engine based on the game UT2003 and then later, UT2004. The toolset provided by the game greatly benefited from the inclusion of Matinee – an interface designed for the scripting of camera edits - and functionality for Character animation. It was hailed as the inclusion of moviemaking functionality in the Unreal Tournament Modding toolset provided by the creators of the game itself.

As a participant in the contest, (I was involved in the contest with two movies) the use of Matinee proved to be essential, but it became clear that its design was lacking flexibility. The overall design philosophy was quite different to that of the Demo-recording days. No live-performance was necessary, but neither was it possible. In addition, camera control and character scripting were separated in the Matinee interface. The only way to test a scene was to "run" the level. This crucial disconnect required a distinct switching from the editing environment to the un-editable game environment in which the camera could be performed, but no positions could be recorded and time could only be slowed down and not otherwise manipulated (no reverse, no fast forward, no jumping to time positions, etc...). While earlier tools like Keygrip were also limited in the way timing could be manipulated for editing, this new way of setting up things via script in an outside tool was even more limited. This made editing decisions and camera placement a lot harder than in "traditional" Machinima environments. On the other hand, the tools included a full Asset importing pipeline for all major 3D content creation tools, a scripting language and plenty of documentation. These provided more options for artistic expression than previous iterations of the engine or other games at the time.

For my contest entry "the Journey" (Kirschner 2004), I created 5 levels that served as scenes for my machinima film, creating custom props, textures, and characters, very similar to creating a game modification. However, my modified landscapes and characters were not meant to be used for play (even though they easily could have been made available as a game level), but as sets in my "real-time non-interactive movie". During production, I realized that a complex setup like this required custom scripts not just for added effects and animation functionality, but also to add organization and structure to the filmmaking process.

Figure 2; The Journey (Kirschner, 2004)

I had to create two sets of modifications. One being the actual Mod that would be my submission for the contest, containing levels, assets and camera scripting. And another one, invisibly intertwined, that helped me create the first one: a set of simple tools that structured my scripting - sometimes as simple as just displaying a dividing line in the list of scripted actions for my characters. Many other participants were performing similar tasks, defining a workflow that would serve Machinima filmmakers as opposed to game modification.

Mods replacing tools

Conversations with other filmmakers engaged in the contest led to much discussion on programming and processes. Some of it was about replacing functionality that was provided by the given toolset, but technically too challenging or cumbersome to use. For example, while the Unreal Engine had a built in tool for facial animation, called "Impersonator", it proved too involved a process to be useful, as described by Eric "Starfury" Bakutis, another entrant in the contest:

> "[...] Impersonator is only useful to a Machinima creator
> if they already have a custom built model that has a fully
> realized facial bone structure, and phoneme animations
> to match... a model of this complexity is currently out
> of reach for the majority of amateur UT2K4 machinima
> makers, and as such, Impersonator is more promise than
> actually useful." (Bakutis, 2004).

157

Bakutis was no stranger to Machinima filmmaking. He was head of the team creating "Devil's Covenant", a major achievement in the Quake movie scene (Bakutis, 1998) and was credited with adding to the official Unreal Development Network documentation (Lin, 2003). His solution was to create his own system for swapping textures on a character model, a way of creating lip-synching animations also used in community toolsets for Quake 2, as discussed earlier. A connection Bakutis acknowledges:

> "Also, my focus is definately[sic] to make this accessible
> to the 'one guy in his garage' audience... I still remember
> the days of Quake2 machinima when just about anybody
> could make a movie without extensive modeling and
> coding backup." (Bakutis, 2004)

In the end, none of the nominees for "Best non-interactive real-time movie" actually used Impersonator. The Impersonator case shows that the existence of sophisticated tools alone does not necessarily translate into actual use, while at the same time the machinima community constantly creates their own modifications, tools and processes to aid the movie-making process. It illustrates that the conception and implementation of machinima tools requires profound knowledge of the machinima process itself, and that machinima filmmaking is in a constant state of redefining its technology and production processes. And modifications play a crucial role in forming and sharing these processes.

Investigating Machinima's potential

My follow up work has investigated the tools and processes for machinima filmmaking in addition to the creative process of actually telling a story. At the time of the "Make Something Unreal Contest", the general belief was that gaming technology, tools and graphical development would lead to a new dawn in machinima filmmaking (Marino in Kirschner, 2004). That tools would get easier to use and more powerful. Or, as put into words by Henry Lowood:

> "It is safe to predict that game developers will soon put robust but easy-to-use machinima tools directly into the hands of an increasing number of players" (Lowood, p.74).

Figure 3; Person 2184 (Kirschner, 2005)

To me, UT2004 was very close to being an ideal machinima production environment. Its shortcomings - described earlier - seemed fixable from a mod-maker's standpoint. For my work, "Person2184" and "the Photographer",

I developed a set of scripts that replaced Matinee and combined camera and character controls (Kirschner, 2004). "Script Composer" was a modification adding to UT2004's editing environment (UnrealEd). It could be used within the UnrealEd environment meaning that it still allowed movies to be distributed as modifications themselves. This "packaged content aspect" as Thain described it, allows the machinima movies to be played back as a level using the game itself – as opposed to a movie file or streaming video. In his text "Machinima as Media", (Nitsche, 2011) Michael Nitsche illustrates the importance of this in defining machinima as its own medium:

> "Game engines provide this real-time rendering as well as other features, including levels of interactivity, that allow dynamic replay of a data file on the local machine of the player audience. 3D modeling programs do not offer such a game-based feature and thus lack the media possibilities associated with it." (Nitsche, 2011, p.120)

As well as being a defining part of machinima filmmaking, this way of distribution also allows for a number of creative possibilities, such as non-deterministic movies that play out differently every time, and on-the-fly modification, as further illustrated by an American Film Institute project that investigated this specific aspect of machinima filmmaking (Nitsche, 2007). It also allows for the examination of the individual assets, levels and scripts, similar to having access to the project files in a 3D animation project as opposed to just watching a rendered movie. This effectively allows remixing of work, and in the case of "Person2184", this aspect was used by students at the University of Plymouth to create original work based on assets I included in my movie:

159

> "We also deconstructed Person2184. [...] We've managed to export some of the characters but they're all in DDS format but with the correct plugin, Photoshop can work with them so we can now see how Friedrich created them." (Saunders, 2006)

According to Nitsche, "Machinima is digital performance that controls procedurally animated moving images." Nitsche does not just talk about real-time playback capabilities but references live interaction and performance as well (Cameron and Carrol in Nitsche, 2011). Real-time performance was impossible within the scope of UnrealEd, given its strict division of the scripting and playback process. The only way to allow for machinima performance within UT2004 while at the same time keeping scripting possibilities, was to create a total conversion modification that would bring UnrealEd's functionality into the actual game aspect of UT2004. Moviesandbox (Kirschner, 2006), was an attempt to do just that. It implemented the same scripting possibilities as scriptcomposer beforehand, retained the "packaged content aspect", but also allowed for live acting and puppeteering of UT2004 characters. I have written about the concepts behind Moviesandbox more extensively (Kirschner, 2011), but want to mention it here as an example of a total conversion modification for machinima filmmaking that tried to follow machinima's potential as voiced by Thain and others, and shared by myself.

Nitsche further argues that, "Whether it was the release of the various editors by id Software, Epic's UnrealEd, or Valve's Source SDK with its Faceposer tool, all helped and empowered the machinima makers, commercial as well as independent. They became the artistic tools for machinima and demo production." (Nitsche, The Machinima Reader, p. 120) I believe this statement is missing a crucial part of machinima's development regarding its Mod heritage. The role of the Machinima filmmakers, and their frustration, in bending and extending the toolsets mentioned is crucial to understanding the turn in development that Machinima was taking. Instead of making extensive use of these advanced toolsets to create more sophisticated and individual movies, the vast majority of machinima filmmakers reverted to

160   their own tools and modifications, that were closer to the initial workflow laid out in the Quake movie era. These workflows ultimately define machinima as "user generated process", a re-framing of given technology into a new medium not just by working within its technical infrastructure, but also by extending it with tools and processes, elevating it to a form of media of its own. This second phase illustrates how the defining factors did not originate from the video-game developers themselves, but were still driven by community effort to shape machinima's form and function.

Phase 3: The current state of Machinima

Bungie's "Halo"(2001), a game for the XBOX console, and Blizzard's "World of Warcraft" (2004) have spawned not just an incredible number of Machinima movies, but also some of the more defining works of the art form. It is safe to say that the potential that others and I saw in it did not reveal itself in the form that Thain or Marino anticipated. The vision of affordable, powerful tools developed by video-game companies that allow for total creative control by expert Machinima filmmakers implemented directly into the games or game tools does not form the basis of Machinima's practice today. Software specifically designed for Machinima creation, such as Moviestorm (Moviestorm, 2007), iClone (Reallusion, 2003) or my own

Moviesandbox (Kirschner, 2006) did not manage to gain the same amount of users, movies, press, or artistic success as the aforementioned games. Machinima.com, the social hub of the game-agnostic machinima online community is not hosting discussion forums anymore. Nitsche clearly agrees that Machinima did not take the route anticipated during the second wave:

> "Popular Machinima practice clearly did not follow the strengths of its own media specifics." (Nitsche, 2011, p.121)

One aspect has not changed over the years since its emergence, however. The perceived deviation from "the strengths of its media specifics" is missing a crucial point of what I see as a fundamental concept in machinima - modding. We know that machinima is tied to the modding scene by its heritage. In fact, Lowood sees machinima as a direct outcome of the Quake modding scene:

> "Not only did providing an editor and scripting language stimulate modification and extension of the game, it encouraged the development of tools for unforeseen purposes, such as the editing of demo movies and, eventually, the making of animated movies using real-time techniques of gameplay as performance." (Lowood, 2005, p.74)

161

But the connection between modifications and machinima is more than just historical. Games like Lionhead's "the Movies" (2005), or Maxis' the Sims 2 provided their own machinima filmmaking features, but were still modded extensively to allow for more creative user choices. The aforementioned "World of Warcraft" spawned a significant amount of modifications and best practices for machinima production. There are many more examples of mods that have spawned machinima movies in games that do not even have any dedicated machinima tools, sometimes by enabling hidden features, sometimes by brute force hacking (Hancock, 2007)

Conclusion

The definition provided by Marino, of machinima as "animated filmmaking within a real-time virtual 3D environment" (Marino, 2004) is a technical definition that does not cover the wider implications of the movement - its commentary and situation within gaming culture. Nitsche's definition as digital performance controlling procedural imagery works against the realities of recent machinima production. Lowood's definition of machinima as "producing animated movies with the software that is used to develop and play computer games" (Lowood, 2008) recognizes machinima's ties to video games, but his notion of machinima as "exploiting found technology" under-represents the role that the modification process plays for machinima as a movement, and the quality of innovation that is generated by the modding and machinima community. None of these definitions emphasize modifications and user generated process as a defining aspect of machinima.

I would like to draw attention to the machinima filmmaker as creator of technology. Mods are a crucial part in the process of machinima to this date, both technically and conceptually. They planted the idea of not only user-generated content, but also user-generated process. At its core, machinima is always going to be a form of game modification. Even when stripped of all of its technological properties and tools, the very idea of using video games for filmmaking is a modification to the rules of most games – and essential to machinima's inception. Machinima will not cease to switch engines and the machinima community will not stop creating modifications and hacks, because it is its very essence to do so. It is part of machinima's transformative power, even hailed as democratization of filmmaking (Matlack, 2005). This user-generated process is a novel way of user innovation that extends beyond modifying media content with tools provided by content creators. Instead, it breaks down provided workflows and established production conventions and establishes a new art form in itself: machinima.

References

Lowood, H. (2008). Found Technology: Players as Innovators in the Making of Machinima. (T. McPherson, Ed.), *Digital Media, Digital Yo,* 165-196. The MIT Press.

Lowood, H., (2005). High-performance play: The making of machinima. (Andy Clarke and Grethe Mitchell Eds.), Videogames and Art: *Intersections and Interactions,* 59-79. Intellect Books.

Hanson, M. (2004). *The End of Celluloid,* 2004, RotoVision.

Kirschner, F. (2004). *Machinimag One.* PDF http://machinimag.com/machinimagOneRe.pdf, retrieved 15.02.2012.

Kirschner, F. (2004). *Machinimag Three.* PDF http://machinimag.com/ machinimagThree.pdf, retrieved 15.02.2012.

Kirschner, F. (2011). Machinima's Promise. *Journal of Visual Culture,* 10(1), 19-24.

Kirschner, F. (2011). Towards a Machinima Studio. (M. Nitsche, H. Lowood, Eds.), *The Machinima Reader,* 54-71. The MIT Press.

Nitsche, M. (2011). Machinima as Media (M. Nitsche, H. Lowood, Eds.), *The Machinima Reader,* 113-125. The MIT Press.

Hancock, H., Ingram, J. (2007). *Machinima for Dummies. For Dummies.*

Marino, P. (2004). *3D Game-Based Filmmaking: The Art of Machinima.* Paraglyph Press.

ILL Clan "Larry and Lenny Lumberjack (movie) (2000).

Kirschner, F. Neumann, K. Scholz, A. "The Bob Block Machinima Show" (live performance) (2004)

Web References

Marino, P. (2005). *Thinking Machinima,* http://www.machinima.org/ paul_blog/2005/10/machinima-from-inside-out.html, retrieved 15.02.1012.

Saunders, C. (2006). *Bit of an Update,* http://www.boxel.co.uk/category/ undergrad/4d/page/2/, retrieved 15.02.2012.

Bakutis, E. (1998). *Devils Covenant (movie),* http://www.tebakutis.com/index_ independent_dc_release.html, retrieved15.02.2012.

Lin, T. (2003). *Sample Matinee Tips,* http://udn.epicgames.com/Two/ SampleMatineeTips.html, retrieved 15.02.2012.

Bakutis, E. (2004). Forum post, http://ataricommunity.com/forums/ showthread.php?p=5397676, retrieved 15.02.2012.

Bakutis, E. (2004). Forum post, http://ataricommunity.com/forums/ showthread.php?t=388116, retrieved 15.02.2012

Press Release NVIDIA Corporation. (2003). *Epic Games and NVIDIA Kick Off "$1,000,000 NVIDIA Make Something Unreal®" Contest. http:// nvidia.com/object/IO_20030606_4169.html,* retrieved 15.02.2012.

Kirschner, F. *The Journey* (movie/game modification). http://journey. machinimag.com, retrieved 15.02.2012 (2004).

Kirschner, F. *Moviesandbox* (software/game modification) (2006). http:// moviesandbox.net, retrieved 15.02.2012.

Nitsche, M. (2007). *American Film Institute goes Machinima*, http://freepixel. org/?p=58, retrieved 15.02.2012.

Matlack, C. (2005). *France: Thousands of Young Spielbergs,* http://www. businessweek.com/magazine/content/05_51/b3964049.htm, retrieved 15.02.2012.

Software References

Quake, ID software 1996

Milkshape 3D, Chumbalum Soft, 1996-

Quake 2, ID software 1997

Unreal Tournament 2003, Epic Games, 2002

Unreal Tournament 2004, Epic Games, 2004

Faceposer, Valve, 2004

3D Studio Max, Autodesk 1995-

the Sims 2, Maxis, 2004

Halo, Bungie, 2001

the Movies, Lionhead, 2005

World of Warcraft, Blizzard, 2004

iClone, Reallusion 2003-

Moviestorm, Moviestorm 2007-

165

CHAPTER 7

CryVE:

Modding the CryEngine2

to create a

CAVE System

167

Marija Nakevska
Alex Juarez
Jun Hu

168

CryVE: Modding the CryEngine2 to create a CAVE system

Marija Nakevska, Alex Juarez, Jun Hu,
Dept. of Industrial Design, Eindhoven University of
Technology, Eindhoven, The Netherlands
m.nakevska@tue.nl, acordova@tue.nl, j.hu@tue.nl

Game engines and game mods

Game engines

A *game engine* is a multiplatform middleware software system that facilitates
game development. Game engines include functionality needed to develop
game applications by using a flexible and reusable software platform. This
helps to reduce costs and complexity in game development. Fundamental
components of modern game engine platforms are a rendering engine for
2D or 3D graphics, and a physics engine for accurate physics simulation.
Other common features are collision detection, sound, scripting, animation,
artificial intelligence, networking, streaming, etc.

An example application of game engines is a *first person shooter (FPS) game.*
A first person shooter (FPS) game is a video game in which the players see
the world from the eyes of their characters and the game revolves primarily
around eliminating or disabling other entities in the game world. A first
person shooter game engine is a game engine specialized for simulating 3D
environments for use in a first-person shooter video game.

Game engines are often used for other kinds of interactive applications
with real-time graphical needs such as marketing demos, architectural
visualizations, training simulations, and modeling environments. As
game engine technology has matured and become more user-friendly, the
application of game engines has also broadened in scope and game engines are
used in visualization, training, medical and military simulation applications.

Game mods

Game engines allow designers to create new game behaviors and graphics by
plugging into reusable architectures that handle polygon rendering, camera
control, lighting and so on. Game engines usually come with scripting

languages that allow users to modify behaviors, create new worlds or modify existing games into completely new ones. Game modifications (generally called mods) are software plugins made by the general public or developer. They can include new items, characters, models, textures, levels, story lines, music and other game mods. Game mods are not standalone software and require the user to have the original game release in order to run.

Commercial game developers have promoted game mods to the community in an "open architecture" approach where partial codes and updates are available to manipulate the game engine. User-created content is usually gathered in knowledge bases for game playing, editing, level (or map) building and distribution. With creating new content and knowledge bases, the community extends and enriches game play experiences. The community also provides free support and tutorials for code alterations, hints for obtaining performance benefits of each other.

Cry Engine

CryEngine is a multiplatform game engine originally developed by Crytek. CryEngine has opened up many possibilities for game designers with its ability to handle extremely large photorealistic interior and vast outdoor spaces while still supporting the scene details (Seeley, 2007).

CryEngine supports a number of features that are useful for creating immersive and realistic games and virtual environments. The necessary development tools are integrated with the engine itself, including *CryEngine Sandbox* world editing system and the Mod SDK that are available as free downloads.

Crysis Mod SDK

Crysis Mod SDK contains tools; assets and game source code to help modders (gamers, hobbyists, and game developers) create their own game mods. The kit includes everything needed to set up a custom modification for *Crysis* and *CryEngine2*, including sample code, tools, mods and assets.

CryEngine Sandbox Editor gives full real-time control to the developers over their multi-platform creations. It introduces a "What You See Is What You Play" (WYSIWYP) system where games can be produced and played immediately. The Sandbox editor is used to create levels for *CryEngine*-based games, and tools are provided within the software to facilitate scripting, animation and object creation.

The foundation for a virtual world is laid by creating a new *map (level)*. Creation and editing of the level and the terrain is facilitated with tools for creating landscape, surface and textures, to which different effects can be applied.

A *Flow Graph* is a simple visual programming system in *CryEngine* that gives designers an intuitive interface to create and control events, triggers, game logic, effects, and sound design. The *Flow Graph System* facilitates the building of complex levels without the need of writing code.

The *Track View* is an editing tool embedded in the *Sandbox Editor* that allows creating cut scenes for making interactive movie sequences. Creating cinematic cut scenes and scripted events can be done in-game by setting a sequence of objects, animations and sounds in a scene which can then be triggered automatically by character interaction. Sequences created with *Track View* can also be triggered in-game with a specific *Flow Graph* node.

CAVE systems

A CAVE system is an immersive virtual reality interface usually consisting of an enclosed environment that surrounds the user with projected images. CAVE systems appeared at the beginning of 1990's as a visualization tool for virtual reality environments that utilized an array of large projection screens, resembling a room whose walls, ceiling and floor showed images specially designed to provide the experience of "immersion" in the virtual world (Cruz-Neira et al., 1992). Since then, several variations of this setup have been developed, examples including asymmetric screens, portable CAVEs with only two walls (Sauter, 2003), arrangements in "U" shape configurations, and semi-spherical screens.

In general, multi-screen immersive systems typically require one or two video outputs for each screen and simultaneously utilize several interaction devices. The capabilities of the CAVE hardware must be assessed before attempting to develop the simulation, as running multiple projections simultaneously requires a fast network and substantial graphical processing. If the network bandwidth is unacceptably low or if the processor speed is inadequate, a distributed CAVE simulation might not be feasible.

Software for CAVE systems has also evolved from research-oriented, custom-made applications that modified the image aspect ratio and display quality, into powerful software tools. Existing solutions are capable of performing high-end 3D modeling and rendering, incorporating multiprocessing and acting as "glue" to other virtual reality components. Other devices can also be incorporated to the system, such as head mounted displays, 3D glasses, pressure and temperature sensors, etc. (Cruz-Neira et al., 2002).

Recently the cost and performance of CAVE systems received a boost with the appearance of game-engine-based virtual reality systems. These systems used commercially available software packages - game engines - that provide advanced simulation and graphics. The most widely known example of this kind of system is CAVEUT (Jacobson & Lewis, 2005, Jacobson 2005), a CAVE based on an extension of the Unreal Engine 2.5 (Unreal technology, 2010). CAVEUT public application programming interface (API) enables users with limited programming experience to build a fully functional CAVE, without having to modify the internal workings of the game engine itself.

A similar CAVE system was reportedly built using the Half-Life Engine (Schou et al. 2007), however, the capabilities, implementation requirements, and costs of such a system were not clearly explained, nor was it clear whether it could currently compete with the graphics, physics and 3D model quality of the Unreal Engine 2.5.

In any case, the constant development of games and game engines results in even more accurate and realistic, state of the art simulation and rendering of virtual environments, all done using commodity hardware. At the same time, current game engines offer the possibility to easily modify and extend the content and behavior of characters and virtual environments through "in-game" editors and public APIs.

Low-cost implementation of a CAVE system

In previous publications, we mentioned that there is a gap in qualitative and quantitative terms between commercial and open source solutions. This gap is the difference between systems that provide stunning visuals, state of the art modeling, rendering and visualization, and continuous support at high costs; and systems that provide cost effective solutions, with more limited visuals, development capabilities, and overall user experience (Nakevska et al., 2011; Juarez et al. 2010).

As a rule of thumb, commercial solutions like the i-Space (Barco Solutions, 2010) or Apollo (HoloVis Cave solutions, 2010) CAVE systems offer accurate and realistic experience customized to the needs of the client, with extensive application and installation support, unfortunately, the cost can be prohibitive. On the other hand, open source, non-commercial solutions like AGAVE (Leigh et al., 2001) and CAVEUT (Jacobson et al., 2005) offer cost-effective setups that are in many cases implemented only at education institutions, using outdated technology, with limited development and scarce support for potential users.

A low-cost implementation is needed to fill in the gap between commercial and open source systems.

The main characteristics of such an implementation would be:

• A low-cost, full-size physical construction. While there are CAVE systems of reduced dimensions at affordable prices, the truly immersive experience comes from a physical setup that can accommodate at least one person standing comfortably, allowing for some space to move and interact with the system.

• Easy to setup, maintain and extend. A system that requires the intervention of experts for even the simplest tasks are unlikely to be more efficient than those where a dedicated enthusiast can get satisfying results. This means that the use of standard and simple components, as well as uncomplicated methods and mechanisms to modify and extend the CAVE are preferred. Furthermore, the existence of an active development community that provides support and continuously improves and extends the software, is also an important factor.

• Realistic immersive experience. A successful CAVE system must provide a believable experience to a spectator, presenting a visually rich virtual environment. The available virtual environment development toolkits provide only a subset of the tools needed to build complete virtual worlds, reusing the computer game technology is alternative for building realistic virtual worlds featuring user-friendly interaction and the simulation of real world.

CryVE CAVE System

CryEngine automatic Virtual Environment (CryVE) is a CAVE system based on the game engine *CryEngine 2*. *CryEngine 2* is game engine developed by the company Crytek. Crytek is founded in 1999, after releasing numerous demos of the game X-Isle, it evolved to the game *Far Cry* and the *CryEngine* that the game uses. In 2007 the game Crysis with the CryEngine 2 was released. The game *Crysis Warhead* as an expansion of *Crysis* was released in 2008 as a PC-exclusive game. The game engine *CryEngine 3* is released on October 2009, in August 2011 Crytek has released *CryEngine 3 Free SDK* package. *CryEngine 3* is free for educational and non-commercial use. Sample assets are included with the *Free SDK*, but also artists, animators and audio engineers can design and export assets to the *CryEngine*.

The software architecture uses the multiplayer features of a *CryEngine* computer game to build projections for the different sides of the installation. The system architecture is similar to that of CAVEUT: multiplayer instances of a *CryEngine 2* game are started on all computers in the system. Computers are connected to each other through a network hub, with one of them acting as a server (master) while the rest are game clients (slaves). The server can control the in-game action (walking, jumping, shooting, etc.) while the clients provide the extra "cameras" that complete the peripheral view required by the CAVE, aligning and synchronizing themselves to the pose and motion of the master.

Finally each computer renders its piece of the virtual world to the corresponding projector and projection screen (see *Figure 1*). In principle any computer game that is based on the *CryEngine 2* can be used in a CryVE setup. Examples of games using *CryEngine 2* are *Crysis, Crysis Warhead, Entropia Universe* and *Blue Mars*.

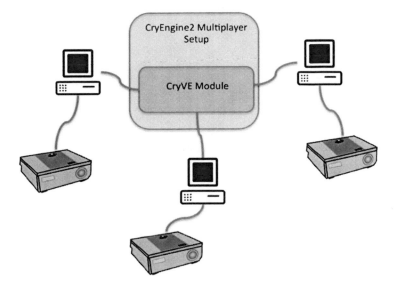

Figure 1; CryVE system architecture.

Physical Setup

The CryVE system physical setup is an arrangement of screens resembling a cubic room, with the projection done from the outside of the room. This allows viewers to move around inside without creating undesired shadows on the projection screens. The installation was built around an aluminum frame that held a plastic white translucent canvas as seen in *Figure 2a*.

Figure 2; Physical installation of the CryVE system.
(Left) Steel frame holding the canvas
(Right) Projectors mounted 4.0 meters above ground

Each side of the room measures 3 X 3 meters and five of the six walls are projecting screens, leaving out only the floor. Each projector is controlled by a single computer, which in turn is connected to a computer network. The first prototype that we created consisted of only three faces of the cube used as projection screens, resulting in a "U" CAVE configuration.

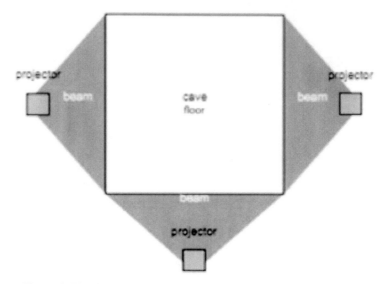

Figure 3; Physical installation of the CryVE system.

The room enclosing the CAVE installation offered a maximum of 2.2 meters of space on each projecting side. Due to this limitation in the physical space available, Hitachi ED-A100 XGA projectors were used. These projectors offer the advantage of a short throwing distance and easy image adjustment to cover the square canvas of the projection screen, albeit at a higher cost than normal projectors. Furthermore, the back projection nature of these devices allowed us to mount them at 4.0 meters above ground outside of the room, enabling free transit around the CAVE without undesired shadows appearing on the canvas (see *Figure 2b*). Each projector was then connected to a computer that controlled one of the projected faces of the room.

Software setup

The CryVE software implementation consists of three components: a game modification (mod), a game Flow Graph and a modified multiplayer map. A *CryEngine 2* game mod is a piece of code (usually written in C++) that can access the low-level data structures and API of the game engine, and extends its functionality by modifying the behavior and appearance of characters, and even the gameplay itself.

The CryVE mod component is in charge of deciding if a specific instance of a game is dedicated as a server or client in the CryVE setup. If the current instance is a master, the mod sends a signal to potential clients (other slaves) that it is available to connect to. If the instance is a client, the mod obtains the camera gaze of the master and aligns the camera view of the client accordingly.

CryVE mod and programming environment of CryEngine

Level setup

Creating the foundation for a virtual world starts with the creation of a new map (level). The *Sandbox editor* facilitates the process of creation of new maps. Using the option *File>New*, the map is created in new folder which contains all the required files. The most important file is the .cry file, which contains all the major information for the editor. Creating and editing of terrain is easily managed by using the option *Terrain>Edit Terrain* which opens the *Generation* window (see *Figure 4*), where the appearance of the terrain can be influenced by setting the parameters: feature size, noise, detail, variation, blurring and sharpness. These parameters determine the amount of land created the deformation of the surface, the random way of seeding of islands, the smoothing or sharpness of the surface.

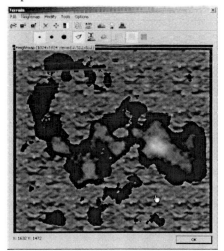

Figure 4; Creating and editing terrain.

The surface texture is easily generated with the option *File > Generate surface texture*. In the *Sandbox editor* more environment setup options are available for modifying terrain: vegetation tool, palette of effects as frozen level or weather effects. The created level can be exported and used in game mode. After creating the virtual world of the game the mission logic can be defined using the *Flow Graph* system in the *Sandbox* editor.

Flow Graph

The *Flow Graph* is a visual scripting system built into the *Sandbox Editor* for the *CryEngine2*. It is used by designers and programmers in creating environment interaction logic. The *Flow Graph* facilitates the process of game development by using visual scripting.

The *Flow Graph* uses nodes to represent entities or behaviors that can be controlled by linking them to other nodes. *Flow Graph* logic is stored in XML format and can be easily exported to disk, in order to be redistributed. A graph is always created and stored on a specific entity which has the benefit of the graph being exported with the object.

A *Graph* is the final result which defines a behavior; it consists of a series of *Nodes* which are *Linked* together via their *Port*.

A *node* is the representation of an entity or an action inside the *Flow Graph*. Node is a container of *Output* and *Input Ports*. There are two categories of nodes: *entity nodes* and *component nodes*.

Entity nodes represent entities, the input and output ports depend on the ports defined in the entity. Component nodes are nodes which can perform special functions but are not related to any entity.

A *node* consists of two sides, an input and an output side, the information transfer of the nodes is handled through *Ports*. *Ports* can send out or receive information. On the left side of a node are input ports used to connect incoming links, links from other nodes are connected into these ports. The ports on the right side of the node are called output ports and are activated depending on the behavior of the node. Ports are represented in the interface as small arrows on both sides of the nodes. Ports can have different data types; the data type is determinate with specific colors. A port can have one of six different types: any, *Boolean, Integer, Float, String, Vec3* (data type consisting of three float values, used to store positions, angles or color values).

Links are used to connect ports and transfer information between them. A *Link* connects an *Output Port* to an *Input Port* between two *Nodes*. Link is visualized as line between the ports of connected nodes.

Flowgraph Plugin System

The modding community provides a number of tools which reduce the labor of making new mods. A big percentage of the modding is based on flow graphs. In order to facilitate the modding process, the *Flowgraph Plugin System* was developed (Crytek, 2011).

The *Flowgraph Plugin System* aims to relive the process of distribution of new custom *Flow Graph* nodes. Previously, a custom mod dll that contained all the new nodes had to be built and this dll had to be distributed to each community member who wished to use the new nodes. The new defined *Flow Graph* nodes are separated into their own lightweight dll files – *plugin*; these *plugins* are detected and loaded by the system automatically merging its contents of *Flow Graph* system into the main system. To use any plugin, the *Flowgraph Plugin System* has to be installed in the relevant *CrysisWars* mod. The *Flowgraph Plugin System* is installed by extracting the Plugin DLLs into *FGPlugin's bin32* and *bin64* folders according to the dll versions. The users have to copy the dlls containing the *Flow Graph* nodes into that folder in the mod directory. To launch the mod in the *Sandbox Editor* the name of the mod has to be included in the path, with preceding –mod (see *Figure 5*). With launching *Sandbox Editor* the included nodes will appear in the *Flow Graph Editor*.

Figure 5; Including a mod in *Sandbox Editor.*

Setting up a programming environment

When the game *Crysis Wars* is installed onto the host pc, the *Software Development Kit Crysis Mod SDK* folder containing the necessary code is automatically created in *C:\Program Files\Electronic Arts\Crytek\CrysisWars\ Mods*. The solution file is located in the folder Code named *GameDll.sln*. Before changing the code it is recommended to copy and rename the *CrysisWarsMod* folder.

In the newly created folder you can find and open *GameDll.sln* solution file in *Visual Studio*, we are using *Visual C++ 2005 Express Edition*.

To set up the properties of the project, right click on the project and *Properties* (see *Figure 6)*, set *Configuration to Active(Debug)*, expand C/C++ section and in *Code Generation* change *Runtime Library* from *Multi-threaded Debug DLL(/ MDd)* to *Multi-threaded)/MT)* and then click *Apply*.

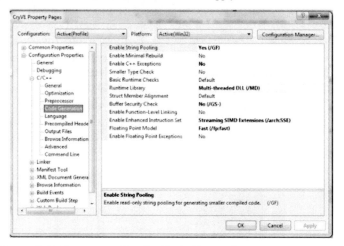

Figure 6; Setting properties for Code Generation.

The path of the output file can be set using the options in *Linker->General (see Figure 7)*

Figure 7; Setting General properties.

Creating a Custom Flow Node

The *CryVE* software uses game modification which aligns the camera view of specific instance of a game as a server or client in the *CryVE* setup. This implementation is done by creating a custom flow node which later will be connected in *Flow Graph*.

181

The custom flow node (*CFlowNode_CryVE*) created for the *CryVE* software has defined specific *Input* and *Output* ports. They are as follows:

Input Ports:

- new config is initialized (*EIP_SetNewConfig*),

- parameter for the name of the config file (*EIP_ ConfigFileName),*

- input when we want to restrict the moving of the camera in different directions (*EIP_FixedCamMode),*

- input when we want to fix the camera orientation (*EIP_FixCurrentCameraOrientation*).

Output Ports: message for multiplayer setup, used as debug message (*EOP_ Message).*

Declaring the Class

After opening the solution file *GameDll.sln* in *Microsoft Visual Studio*, a new source file *CryVE.cpp* should be created in the *Nodes* filter of the *GameDll* project. More header files need to be included:

> *#include "StdAfx.h"*
>
> *#include "GameRules.h"*
>
> *#include "GameCVars.h"*
>
> *#include "Player.h"*
>
> *#include "Nodes/G2FlowBaseNode.h"*
>
> *#include <string>*
>
> *#include <fstream>*
>
> *#include <iostream>*

The precompiled header file and the *Nodes/G2FlowBaseNode.h* file define a class *CFlowBaseNode* which aids in creating a custom flow node.

The defined class *CFlowNode_CryVE* inherits the *CFlowBaseNode* class and overloads a few member functions to handle the logic behind the node. We will define the following member functions:

Constructor

> *Signature: Constructor(SActivationInfo* pActInfo)*

The Constructor will need to take in a *SActivationInfo** as its only argument. The constructor is usually used for handling the member variables that have been defined.

Destructor

> *Signature: virtual Destructor(void)*

GetConfiguration

> Signature: void GetConfiguration(SFLowNodeConfig

&config)

This member function is called by the *Flow Graph System* to get the information about the node from the *Flow Graph Editor*. The argument config is an out variable and is used to supply the info about the node for the system.

ProcessEvent

*Signature: void ProcessEvent(EFlowEvent event, SActivationInfo *pActInfo)*

This member function will be called whenever an event needs to be handled and implements the functions of the node. Such events include its initialization and when a port becomes active or a key is pressed, what means we have to load different configuration. The event argument gives information about the event and *pActInfo* pass the information needed to handle the event.

Setting up the Configuration

Configuration of a node includes information about what *Input* and *Output* ports it has, the default values for any *Input Ports, Help strings* for the node and the ports, the default values for any *Input Ports* used to hold data.

GetConfiguration routine handles the default values and help strings. *SFlowNodeConfig* is one argument of *GetConfiguration* routine; this object has two member variables that allow specifying the input and output ports. These member variables are pointers to a data type *SInputPortConfig* and *SOutputPortConfig*. The ports are defined into two separate arrays, one for input and one for output ports and then supplied to the config object.

The *Ports* are defined in array format and each port has own index value in the array, the *portIDs* are defined in enumeration object and have to be in the same order. Two enumeration objects *EInputPorts* and *EOutputPorts* are declared to hold the index values of the ports. Using the ports defined from the beginning, the enumeration is:

Examples:
```
enum INPUTS {
    EIP_SetNewConfig = 0,
    EIP_ConfigFileName,
    EIP_FixedCamMode,
```

```
EIP_FixCurrentCameraOrientation
};
enum OUTPUTS
{
EOP_Message
};
```

The signatures of the template *InoutPortConfig* and *OutputPortConfig*
functions are as followed:

Examples:

InputPortConfig<type> (Name, HelpString, HumanName, UIConfig)

InputPortConfig<type> (Name, DefaultValue, HelpString, HumanName, UIConfig)

InputPortConfig_Void (Name, HelpString, HumanName, UIConfig)

The *Port* arrays in *GetConfiguration* routine have to be static. Required
arguments when defining a port are *Name* and *Default Value*. Help string is
not mandatory but it is recommended, it helps when working with the node
in the *Flow Graph Editor.*

Default Value argument is used to assign a default value to the port. This
argument is used by setting the port to a common value which helps the
user in the *Flow Graph Editor.* If this argument holds a string value, then all
the next arguments have to be defined to at least NULL value otherwise the
compiler may confuse the *Default Value* argument with *Help String* argument
or it can throw an ambiguity error.

HelpString argument is used to define the help message the user will get in
the *Flow Graph Editor* when hover the mouse over the port. This argument is
not required but it is recommended to use a description which will explain the
purpose of the port.

Example: _HELP("Call to do something!")

HumanName argument is used to specify a more human like name for the
port used in the *Flow Graph Editor.*

Example: _HELP("My Port")

With the argument *UIConfig* an enumeration of possible values can be
specified and the user can select one of those values when setting the value of
the port. Enumeration is used when set of choices is limited and presented as a

list instead of free value.

Example: _UICONFIG("enum_int:On=1,Off=0")

Category of the node can be defined with using the function config. *SetCategory()* to filter the nodes which can be used in the *FlowGraph Editor*. The valid categories which can be set and they generally stand for: *EFLN_APPROVED, EFLN_ADVANCED, EFLN_DEBUG, EFLN_WIP, EFLN_LEGACY, EFLN_NOCATEGORY*. Depending on the set category the node can be approved and guaranteed to work *(EFLN_APPROVED)*, labeled as advanced *(EFLN_ADVANCED)*, used only for debugging purposes *(EFLN_DEBUG)*, considered a Work in progress (EFLN_WIP), outdated and will be deleted *(EFLN_LEGACY)*, or it can be labeled as no category *(EFLN_NOCATEGORY)*.

The *GetConfiguration* routine will be defined as:

```
void GetConfiguration( SFlowNodeConfig& config )
{
        static const SInputPortConfig inputs[] =
        {
                InputPortConfig<bool>("SetNewConfig",false,_HELP("New configuration")),

                InputPortConfig<string>("ConfigFilename", _HELP("Name config. file.")),

                InputPortConfig<bool>("FixedCameraMode", _HELP("Fixed camera.")),

                InputPortConfig<bool>("FixCurrentCameraOrientation", _HELP("")),

                {0}
        };

        static const SOutputPortConfig outputs[] =
        {
                OutputPortConfig<string>("Message", _HELP("Debug message")),

                {0}
        };
```

```
config.pInputPorts = inputs;

config.pOutputPorts = outputs;

config.sDescription = _HELP("FG node that sets up a CAVE environment");

config.SetCategory(EFLN_APPROVED);
```

/

Handling the Events

ProcessEvent member function defines the logic for handling the events of the node. This routine has an event argument of type *EFlowEvent*. The datatype EFlowEvent is an enumeration with events most important arguments are:

- *eFE_Update* event, called when the node is updated.

- *eFE_Activate* event, called when one or more Input Ports are active.

- *eFE_FinalActivate,* has the same function as eFE_ Activate but is called after eFE_Update.

- *eFE_Initialize* event, called after the level has been loaded, then some basic initialization can be done.

The event argument can be wrapped in a switch statement and the events can be handled in case statements. *IsPortActive* is a helper function which gives information if the referred port is active.

In the CryVE setup we want to create a node which - depending on the configuration - will decide if a specific instance of a game is a server or client. Then the system is calibrated accordingly; if the current instance is a master, the mod sends a signal to potential clients (other slaves) that it is available to connect. If the instance is a client, the mod obtains the gaze of the master and aligns the camera view of the client accordingly. Once the cameras are aligned, CryVE reads a configuration file for the required image transformation (place translation, rotation and frustum shape transformation in 3D space).

In order to calibrate the system appropriately, there are some parameters that must be calculated depending on the geometry of the CAVE and the desired viewing position inside it. These parameters are the field of view (FOV), yaw, pitch, and roll of the projection. M. Penna (M. Penna, 1991) showed that the yaw, pitch and roll parameters for the perspective projection of a quadrilateral can be calculated using

$$\alpha = tan^{-1}\left(\frac{r_{12}}{r_{11}}\right)$$

$$\beta = tan^{-1}\left(-\frac{r_{13}}{(r_{11}^2 + r_{12}^2)^{\frac{1}{2}}}\right)$$

$$\gamma = tan^{-1}\left(\frac{r_{23}}{r_{33}}\right)$$

where r_x are the components of a 3 X 3 matrix that defines the desired rigid motion rotation of the projection plane.

As the prototype implementation is a cubic CAVE, the desired point of view was fixed at the center of the cube. This simplifies the calculation of the camera look view parameters, resulting in

$$\alpha = \frac{\pi}{2}$$

$$\beta = 0$$

$$\gamma = 0$$

The calculation of the vertical and horizontal FOV is done by applying the formula, where H and W are height and width of the cube, respectively

$$FOV_{vertical} = 2\theta = \left(tan^{-1}\left(\frac{H}{2p}\right)\right)$$

$$FOV_{horizontal} = 2\varphi = 2\left(tan^{-1}\left(\frac{W}{2p}\right)\right)$$

However, given the cubic shape of the CAVE, we know that $FOV_{vertical} = FOV_{horisontal}$. Furthermore, we observe that p = W/2 = H/2, therefore, the formula for FOV (both horizontal and vertical) can be simplified to

$$FOV = 2\left(tan^{-1}\left(\frac{H}{2p}\right)\right) = 2(tan^{-1}\left(\frac{W}{2p}\right)$$

$$FOV = 2(tan^{-1}(1))$$

$$FOV = \pi/2$$

The calculation of the parameters for each face of the cube is done in a similar way. After this, the process of translation and rotation is applied to each image frame before it is rendered by the clients. Figure 8 shows the process diagram for the CryVE mod.

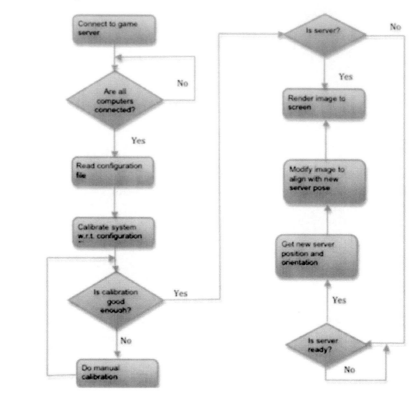

Figure 8; CryVE mod process diagram.

Registering with the Flow Graph System

The created custom Flow Node has to be registered to be used in the Flow Graph Editor. The system handles the node class according to which register macro is chosen. We are using REGISTER_FLOW_NODE macro with this registration, a new instance of the node is created each time it is used in a graph.

> REGISTER_FLOW_NODE("Multiplayer:CryVESetup", CFlowNode_CryVE);

Other register macros which can be used to register the node

- *REGISTER_FLOW_NODE_SINGLETON,* uses a single instance of the class for all occurrences of the node regardless of where it is used.

- *REGISTER_FLOW_NODE_EX, REGISTER_ FLOW_NODE_SINGLETON_EX* are extended registration methods and should be used if the node class is a template.

Using the Node in the Editor

According to registration of the node above, we can find it in the *Flow Graph Editor* under *Multiplayer/SetupCryVE.*

The *CryVE Flow Graph* can encapsulate the libraries produced by the mod into a component that can be reused in any *CryEngine 2* game. *The Flow Graph* defines input and output ports for the mod and connects them to other in game components, such as *player_HUD (Head-Up Display), player_id, player_position, and player_stance. Figure 9* shows the resulting *Flow Graph* in the *CryVE* plugin, along with other components and *Flow Graphs* already available in the game engine.

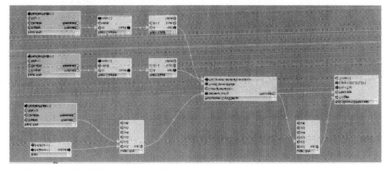

Figure 9; CryVE prototype Flow Graph.

Every *Flow Graph* must be encapsulated in a map for it to be used within a game. In a previous academic publication (Nakevska et al., 2011) we presented several case studies that ran as a mixed reality environment. For the needs of every application, a map is created, which also contains the *Flow Graph* and mod implementations. The map has to be installed in all the computers in the network.

A Virtual Museum Tour

We developed a conceptual design of a Virtual Museum Exhibition that show-cased historic events from the Netherlands (Juarez et al., 2009). The virtual environment resembled a medieval settlement, a virtual world that recreated sixteenth century Holland (see *Figure 10*). For this, a medieval game map was modified by adding dynamic interactions that could be selected by the visitors, leading to the main historic event. Visitors of the museum can use a portable controller in combination with CryVE to have an immersive experience. Using a handheld device, the visitor walks through the landscape and meets people (avatars) with whom he or she can interact. The handheld device is used as interface for interaction and in a subtle way it will introduce the visitor to the historic event that is about to happen in the virtual world. Other museum visitors can also join the exhibition. Each visitor has their own audio, and is able to select their own interaction with people in the virtual world through the handheld device. Having separate audio and shared visuals in the virtual world, allows visitors to have both individual and group experiences, and at the same time, it enables them to interact with people and objects in the virtual environment.

Figure 10; A tour in the Virtual Museum.

Virtual Garden with tangible interfaces

The Virtual Garden project is an attempt at aiding a layperson to design his or her garden, without requiring the user to be proficient with computers. A CryEngine-driven CAVE is used to create a convincing virtual environment. The user can explore and manipulate this environment through a tangible interface, which is basically a miniature representation of the virtual environment (see *Figure 11*). Because of this direct mapping between objects of the interface and of the visualization, users of the installation can understand the interaction and start to explore the virtual environment instantly. The current prototype is implemented using existing visualization and VR techniques. The physical objects of the interface are fitted with pattern markers and are tracked by a webcam from underneath the objects. The position and rotation of the object from the video stream are written to an XML file where each of the objects is a child with three attributes (xpos, ypos, rotation). This XML file is subsequently read out by the game engine, which dynamically updates the positions of the objects in the virtual environment according to the acquired position data using a custom handler.

Figure 11; Impression of the Virtual Garden.

Conclusion

We presented *CryVE, CryEngine 2* game modification software which creates the new *Flow Graph* node needed to enable the *CryEngine* to be used as underlying software for a CAVE system. We presented the tools and methods needed for development of this kind of modification and the advantages of using game engine as an alternative in building virtual and mixed reality environments. With CryVE system we have created a platform for easily development of virtual environments; our challenge in the near future is to develop platforms which will easily integrate different inputs from mixed reality environments. Problems which have to be solved are synchronization of the frame buffers, integration of different input devices and flexibility in incorporation of different sensors, actuators and input/output devices.

References

Barco Solutions (2011). i-space cave system: Multi-walled stereoscopic environment. Retrieved from *http://www.barco.com/en/product/732*

Cruz-Neira, C., Sandin, D., DeFanti, T., Kenyon, R., & Hart, J. (1992). The CAVE: audio visual experience automatic virtual environment. *SIGGRAPH*, June 1992.

Cruz-Neira, C., Bierbaum, A., Hartling, P., Just, C., & Meinert, K. (2005). VR juggler-an open source platform for virtual reality applications. *40th AIAA Aerospace Sciences Meeting and Exhibit.*.

Crytek (2011). Cryengine2 Specifications. Retrieved from http://crytek.com/cryengine/cryengine2/overview.

Flowgraph Plugin System for Crysis-Wars (2011). Retrieved from http://fgps.sourceforge.net/Help/main.html

HoloVis, Cave solutions (2011). Apollo CAVE solutions: Saving time and money through immersive visualizations. Retrieved from http://www.holovis.com/pdf/HoloVisCAVE.pdf

Jacobson, J. & Lewis, M. (2005). Game Engine Virtual Reality with CaveUT. *IEEE Computer 38 (4)*, 79–82.

Jacobson, J., Le Renard, M., Lugrin, J., & Cavazza, M. (2005). The CaveUT system: immersive entertainment based on a game engine. *Proceedings of the 2005 ACM SIGCHI International Conference on Advances in computer entertainment technology*, ACM, 187.

Juarez, A., Schonenberg, W., Bartneck, C. (2011). LIVE HISTORY - a vision for the National Historic Museum in Arnhem, Netherlands. Retrieved from http://nhm.id.tue.nl.

Juarez, A., Schonenberg, B., & Bartneck, C. (2010). Implementing a Low-Cost CAVE system using the CryEngine2. *Journal of Entertainment Computing*, Vol1, Issue 3-4. Elsevier, Dec. 2010, 157-164.

Nakevska, M., Vos, C., Juarez, A., Hu, J., Langereis, G. & Rauterberg, M.

(2011). Using Game engines in mixed reality installations. *10th International Conference on Entertainment Computing*, Vancouver, Canada, 2011.

Penna, M. (1991). Determining camera parameters from the perspective projection of a quadrilateral. *Pattern Recognition*, 24 (6), 533–541.

Leigh, J., Dawe, G., Talandis, J., He, E., Venkataraman, S., Ge, J., Sandin, D. & DeFanti, T. (2001). Agave: Access grid augmented virtual environment. Proc. *AccessGrid Retreat*, Argonne, Illinois.

Sauter, P. M. (2003), Vr2go: a new method for virtual reality development. *SIGGRAPH Comput. Graph. 37* (1) (2003) 19–24. Retrieved from doi:http://doi.acm.org/10.1145/763993.763995.

Schou, T., Gardner, H. (2007). A Wii remote, a game engine, five sensor bars and a virtual reality theatre. *Proceedings of the 19th Australasian conference on Computer-Human Interaction: Entertaining User Interfaces, ACM*, 234.

Seeley, H. (2007). Game technology 2007: Cryengine2. *ACM SIGGRAPH 2007 Computer Animation Festival, ACM*, 64.

Unreal technology (2010). Retrieved from http://www.unrealengine.com/features

Contributors

Dr. Erik Champion is currently Project Leader of the new Digital Humanities Lab Denmark, hosted at Aarhus University in Denmark. Previously an Associate Professor and Director of Research and Postgraduate Studies at the Auckland School of Design, Massey University, in New Zealand, he has taught game design, interaction design, and design history, and researches in the area of virtual heritage and serious games.

Peter Christiansen is currently a PhD student at the University of Utah, where he teaches courses in Videogame Studies and New Media. He is an avid videogame player, prolific doodler and occasional blogger, whose research interests lie in videogame rhetoric, game design and the Independent Games Movement. He has been making games professionally since 2005, but has yet to be employed by a traditional development studio. He is currently employed by ASPIRE, the outreach program for the Utah High Energy Astrophysics Institute, where he develops educational Flash games to teach children physics. He has also worked on a number of independent projects, including several entries for game-in-a-day competitions. He lives in Salt Lake City with his wife and son.

Kevin Conway took several years off from professional practice to pursue his interest in the use of virtual environments as a means of understanding architecture. He researches in the area of virtual architecture and design, digital architecture and design computing. Kevin is currently a senior project manager at a Seattle architecture and design firm.

Dr. Eric Fassbender's general interests are in virtual heritage, the use of virtual environments for teaching purposes and the role that music plays in affecting our learning performance. Most recently Eric has become interested in the use of mobile devices for museum tours as well as the use of immersive environments for relaxation purposes to improve general wellbeing of hospital patients and people at home.

Dr. Jun Hu has a PhD in Industrial Design and a Professional Doctorate in User-system Interaction, both from Eindhoven University of Technology (TU/e). He has also a B.Sc in Mathematics and a M.Eng in Computer Science. He is now a tenured Assistant Professor at Department of Industrial Design, TU/e, a Guest Professor at School of Digital Media, Jiangnan University. He is an Associate Editor of the International Journal of Arts and Technology. He is an author of several open source and commercial software products. He has about 80 peer reviewed publications in conferences and journals in the field of HCI, industrial design, computer science and design education. His current research activities are directed towards Design Research on Social Computing.

Dr. Alex Juarez has a PhD in Industrial Design, obtained at Eindhoven University of Technology. His background is on Computer Science (BSc. in Computer Science) and robotics (MSc. in Autonomous Systems). During his PhD he studied the interaction between virtual worlds and real robots, contributing to the creation of a new communication standard for virtual worlds MPEG-V. He is the creator of the original CryVE system, and together with Dr. Christoph Bartneck and Willem Schonenberg he used CryVE to recreate 13th century Holland as part of an interactive virtual museum tour. Since 2012 he has been working at ASML, the world leader in lithography products for the semiconductor industry. He was appointed as a Metrology Design Engineer and is currently busy developing the next generation of machines that manufacture smaller, faster, and greener integrated circuits.

Friedrich Kirschner is Professor for digital media in the University of Performing Arts "Ernst-Busch" in Berlin. He re-purposes computer games and realtime animation technology to create animated narratives and interactive performances. His work has been shown at various international animation festivals and exhibitions, including the Laboral Gameworld exhibit in Gijon, the American Museum of the Moving Image in New York, the Ottawa international Animation festival and the Seoul Media Art Biennale.

Marija Nakevska is a PhD candidate at the Department of Industrial Design at the TU Eindhoven. She graduated with a major in Computer Science from the Institute of Informatics - Faculty of Natural Sciences and Mathematics - Saints Cyril and Methodius University, Skopje, Macedonia. She has several years working experience in the fields of software engineering, information systems modeling and design, system integration, distributed systems, databases and web technologies. She joined the Designed Intelligence group in August 2010, her current research is part of the project ALICE which aims to provide an experimental platform for achieving certain types of user experiences with mixed reality.

Dr. Natalie Underberg is Associate Professor of Digital Media and Folklore in the University of Central Florida School of Visual Arts and Design (SVAD). She received her B.A. in Anthropology from U.C. Berkeley, and her M.A. and Ph.D. in Folklore from Indiana University. Her research examines the use of digital media to preserve and disseminate folklore and cultural heritage, with a focus on ethnographic storytelling and collaborative methods of employing new media. Her publications include articles in journals including the Journal of American Folklore, Folklore, Visual Anthropology Review, and International Digital Media Arts Journal. In addition, she is lead author on a book on Digital Ethnography to be published in Spring 2013 by the University of Texas Press. She has been PI or co-PI on grants totaling nearly $140,000. Her research has been presented at 14 national and international conferences, including the Bilan du Film Ethnographique seminar in Paris, France and the Digital Humanities Conference in Oulu, Finland (co-author). Dr. Underberg spent the 2011-2012 academic year on sabbatical in Peru, conducting ethnographic research on cultural heritage and tourism on Peru's North Coast and teaching graduate coursework in the Pontifical Catholic University of Peru-Lima's Visual Anthropology M.A. program.